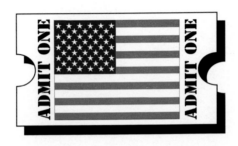

Sunrise On The United States Capitol In Washington D.C.

FACES
AND
PLACES

THE UNITED STATES

BY KATHRYN STEVENS

THE CHILD'S WORLD®, INC.

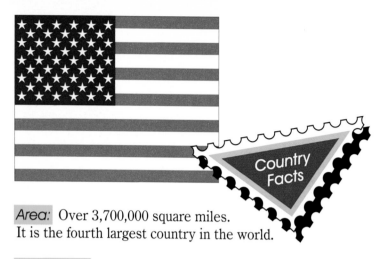

Country Facts

Area: Over 3,700,000 square miles.
It is the fourth largest country in the world.

Population: Over 265 million people.

Capital City: Washington, D. C.

Other Important Cities: Boston, Chicago, Dallas, Detroit, Houston, Los Angeles, Miami, New York, Philadelphia, San Francisco.

Money: The dollar. One dollar is made up of 100 cents.

National Flag: The "Stars and Stripes." The flag's 13 red and white stripes stand for the original 13 colonies. Its blue rectangle has 50 white stars that stand for the nation's 50 states.

National Holiday: Independence Day on July 4.

National Anthem: "The Star-Spangled Banner."

Official Name: The United States of America.

Head of Government: The president of the United States of America.

Library of Congress Cataloging-in-Publication Data
Stevens, Kathryn, 1954-
The United States / by Kathryn Stevens
Series: "Faces and Places".
p. cm.
Includes index.
Summary: Describes the United States, it's geography, history, people, and customs.
ISBN 1-56766-602-7 (library : reinforced : alk. paper)

1. United States — Juvenile literature.
[1. United States] I. Title.

E156.S75 1999
973 — dc21

98-47673
CIP
AC

GRAPHIC DESIGN
Robert A. Honey, Seattle

PHOTO RESEARCH
James R. Rothaus / James R. Rothaus & Associates

ELECTRONIC PRE–PRESS PRODUCTION
Robert E. Bonaker / Graphic Design & Consulting Co.

PHOTOGRAPHY
Cover photo: Portrait of Young African-American Girl by Laura Dwight/Corbis

Table of Contents

If you could fly high above Earth, you would see large areas of land that are mostly surrounded by water. These huge land areas are called **continents**. The United States of America lies on the continent of North America.

Western Hemisphere

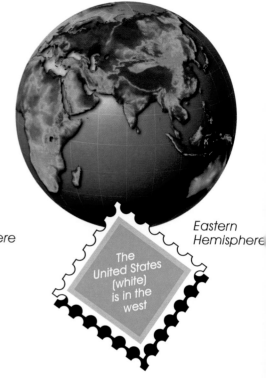

Eastern Hemisphere

The United States (white) is in the west

The main part of the United States stretches from the Atlantic Ocean on the east to the Pacific Ocean on the west.

Its two neighbors are Canada to the north and Mexico to the south. The main area contains 48 of the nation's 50 states.

The state of Alaska is far up in North America's northwest corner, on the other side of Canada. The state of Hawaii is a string of islands far out in the Pacific Ocean.

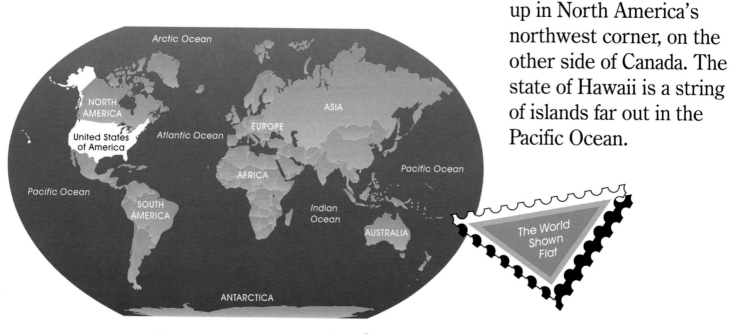

The World Shown Flat

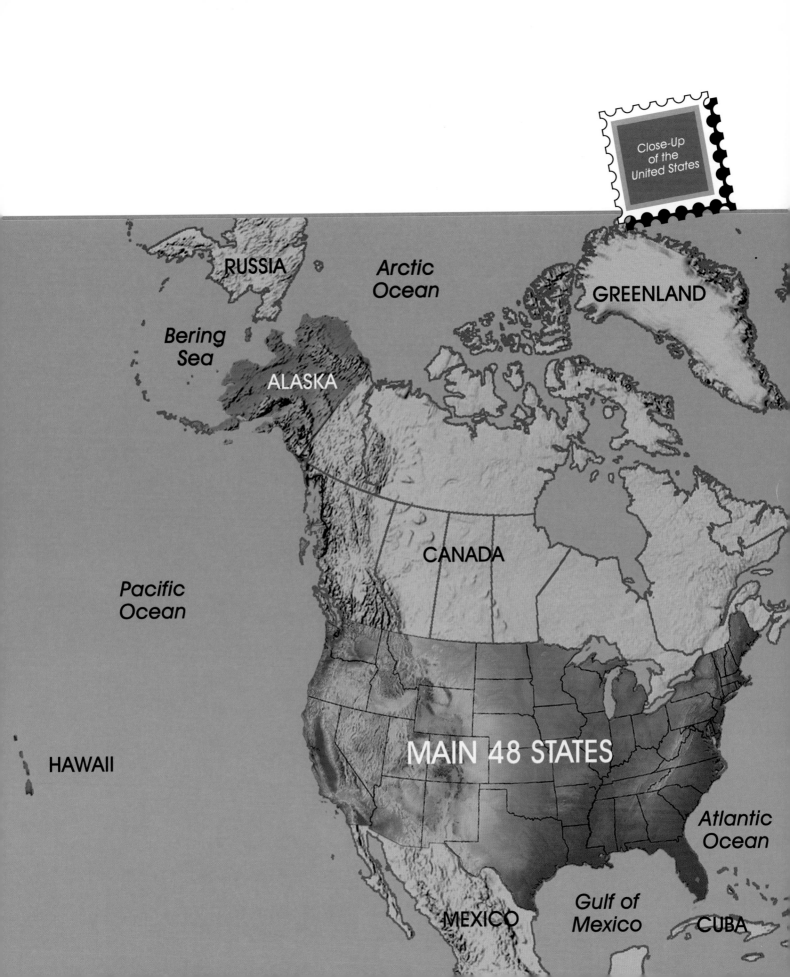

The Island
Of Kauai Is
The Rainiest
Place
On Earth

CANADA

ALASKA

Mount
+ McKinley

Kauai

HAWAIIAN
ISLANDS

WEST COAST

CASCADES

SIERRAS

ROCKY MOUNTAINS

DESERT
AREA

Monument
Valley

GREAT
PLAINS

Great
Lakes

New York

Washington D.C.
Stony Man Mountain

APPALACHIAN MOUNTAINS

EAST COAST

FLORIDA

Douglas Peebles/Corbis

Monument Valley In The Desert Area

David Muench/Corbis

The United States is the world's fourth-largest country. Along the East Coast is a flat area, called a **coastal plain**, with important cities such as New York and Washington, D.C. Just to its west are the rounded, scenic Appalachian (app-uh-LAY-chun) Mountains. The Great Lakes lie at the nation's northern edge, next to Canada. Much of the central United States is taken up by the broad, flat Great Plains. Farther to the west lie the jagged, beautiful Rocky Mountains. The West Coast has mountains, too, including the Sierra Nevada mountains and the Cascades.

Both the land and the weather within the United States vary tremendously. The Hawaiian Islands and some southern regions, such as Florida, are hot and moist. The southwestern states are hot and dry, with many **desert** areas that get very little rain.

The northern states have colder weather, with long winters and lots of snow. Parts of Alaska, the northernmost state, are so cold that the ground is frozen solid all year long!

© Kennan Ward/Corbis

Mt. McKinley Is The Highest Place In The U.S.

Stony Man Mountain In The Appalachians

Jim Richardson/Corbis

Caribou On The Tundra In Alaska

©Kennan Ward/Corbis

The nation's plants and animals vary as widely as its land and weather. The East Coast, Appalachian Mountains, and other regions once had dense forests full of deer, bears, and other wildlife. Many of these forests have been replaced by towns and farms. The Great Plains were once covered by grasslands called **prairies**, where millions of bison roamed. Much of this region is now used for farming and grazing.

The western mountains and valleys were also filled with wildlife, including bears, elk, and deer. Some of this wildlife still remains.

Alaska and Hawaii have some very different plants and animals. Alaska's colder areas have short grasslands called **tundra**. Caribou (KARE–ih–boo), polar bears, and other Alaskan animals live there. Hawaii, on the other hand, has warm, wet weather all year round. Beautiful flowers and colorful birds live in its warm, green forests.

Layne Kennedy/Corbis

Black Bear In Minnesota Forest

Alligator In Everglades National Park, Florida

W. Perry Conway/Corbis

ALASKA

HAWAII

MINNESOTA

GREAT PLAINS

KANSAS

APPALACHIAN MOUNTAINS

EAST COAST

FLORIDA

Everglades National Park

Bison
In Kansas
On The
Great Plains

Philip Gould/Corbis

ALASKA

UTAH
Cliff Dwellings

NEW YORK
• White Plains

VIRGINIA
• Jamestown

GEORGIA
Albany •

EAST COAST

Acting Out
The 1776
Revolutionary
War Battle In
White Plains,
New York

Ted Spiegel/Corbis

We often say that Christopher Columbus and other European explorers "discovered" the land that is now America, but that is not really true. Many people were already living there! Thousands of years earlier, people crossed from Asia to Alaska and spread throughout North and South America. These Native Americans hunted, grew crops, and lived in camps, villages, or towns.

When the Europeans arrived, they accidentally brought diseases that killed many native peoples. The new settlers also bought or simply took the native people's lands. European nations claimed the new regions as **colonies**—lands ruled by the distant European governments. England ruled the 13 colonies along the East Coast.

Jamestown, Virginia Was First English Settlement (1607)

Richard T. Nowitz/Corbis

Eventually, the people who lived in these colonies rebelled against their British rulers. They fought a war for independence called the *American Revolution.* In 1783 the rebels won, and the United States of America became a free nation.

Kevin Fleming/Corbis

Anasazi Cliff Dwellings In Utah Are 700 Years Old

Remembering The Past, A Cherokee Man Attends A Festival In Albany, Georgia

David Muench/Corbis

Iolani Palace
In Honolulu
Now Houses
The Hawaiian
State
Legislators

Over time, more and more of North America was added to the United States. In 1860 and 1861, eleven southern states tried to break away and form a new nation called the *Confederate States of America*. After a bitter war called the *Civil War* and many deaths, the Confederacy was defeated in 1865, and the southern states rejoined the United States. Later, new Western states were added to the nation. The last two states to join were Alaska and Hawaii in 1959.

Today the United States is the most powerful nation in the world. The American people hold elections and vote to decide who the nation's leaders will be. For many years the United States and the Soviet Union were the world's two strongest countries. The Soviet Union split into a number of smaller countries in the early 1990s. Since then, the United States has been considered the most powerful country in the world.

The World Trade Center And United Nations Are In Manhattan, New York City

Richard T. Nowitz/Corbis

NEW YORK

New York City

PENNSYLVANIA

Gettysburg

ALASKA

★ Honolulu

HAWAII

Acting Out
The 1863
Civil War
Battle Of
Gettysburg,
Pennsylvania

Mardi Gras
In The
French
Quarter Of
New Orleans,
Louisiana

NEW YORK
New Brunswick • Ellis Island
NEW JERSEY

San Francisco

CALIFORNIA

LOUISIANA

New Orleans

America has been called a "melting pot" of people from all over the world. First came the continent's earliest settlers, the Native Americans. Next came European settlers from Great Britain, France, and Spain. Newcomers also came from other European countries such as Germany, Italy, and Russia. Newcomers who move to one country from another are called **immigrants**.

People have immigrated to the United States from other regions as well, including Asia, the Middle East, Africa, and Central and South America. Most immigrants hoped to make better lives for themselves. Others did not come by choice. **Slavery**, or "owning" other people, was once a common practice. Many African people were captured and brought to the United States as slaves. Slavery was outlawed in 1863 when President Abraham Lincoln signed the Emancipation Proclamation. Most African-Americans descended from the freed slaves.

Now A Museum, Ellis Island, New York, Opened For Immigrants In 1892

Bill Ross/Corbis

Bob Krist/Corbis

African American Professor At Rutgers University, New Brunswick, New Jersey

Chinese New Year, Lion Dance, In San Francisco, California

Mark Stephenson/Corbis

ADMIT ONE

City Life
And
Country
Life

ADMIT ONE

Rows Of Apartment Houses In Boston, Massachusetts

Reinhard Eisele/Corbis

About three-quarters of America's people live in large cities, called **urban** areas. The cities are surrounded by smaller communities called **suburbs**. America's cities are busy, active places with high-rise buildings, bustling shopping and office areas, and streets filled with cars and buses. Many city-dwellers live in houses, while others live in apartment buildings. Some urban neighborhoods are wealthy, but others are poor and run down.

The American countryside has thousands of small towns. Outside the towns, people still live on farms or in single houses scattered across the countryside. Throughout the 1900s, the population of many of these country, or **rural**, areas has dropped as more people have moved to the cities.

People Live In Houseboats On Portage Bay, Seattle, Washington

Morton Beebe, S. F./Corbis

Nik Wheeler/Corbis

A Wealthy House In Beverly Hills, California

Julie Habel/ Corbis

Seattle• WASHINGTON

MASSACHUSETTS ☆ Boston

IOWA •Millville

CALIFORNIA

•Beverly Hills

Country
Farm
Outside Of
Millville,
Iowa

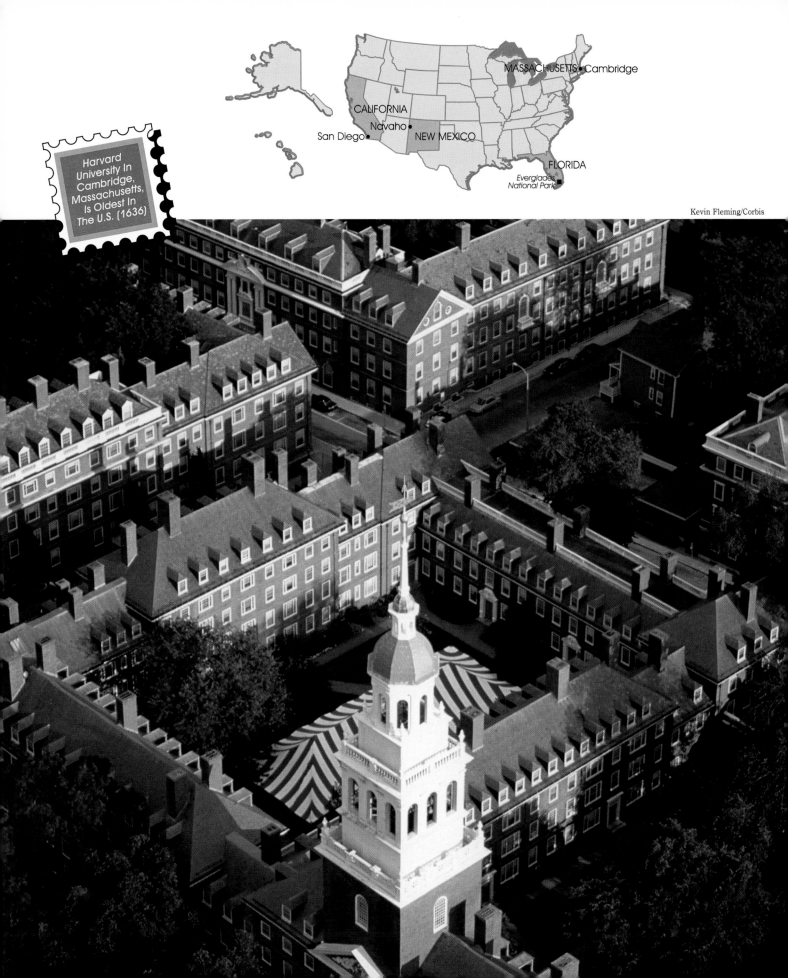

Harvard University In Cambridge, Massachusetts, Is Oldest In The U.S. (1636)

MASSACHUSETTS • Cambridge

CALIFORNIA

Navaho •

San Diego • NEW MEXICO

FLORIDA

Everglades National Park •

Schools And Language

All American children are required to go to school. They attend primary school for six to eight years. There they learn reading, writing, math, and other subjects. Then they go on to middle school or junior high, and to high school. Most students finish high school, with their last year being grade 12. Many then go to a college or university.

English is the most widely used language in the United States. Some Americans also speak the languages of their native cultures. Spanish is a commonly spoken language. Many other languages are spoken as well, including Russian, German, Norwegian, Chinese, Japanese, Vietnamese, Arabic, and Native American languages.

Students Learning About Jungle Life In San Diego, California

Jim Sugar Photography/Corbis

Everglades Park Ranger Teaches About Wildlife

Jim Sugar Photography/Corbis

Teacher Helps Student At Navaho School In New Mexico

Kevin Fleming/Corbis

Work

The traditional American work week is eight hours a day, five days a week—a total of 40 hours each week. In reality, many people work either shorter or longer hours. Some people work at two or even three different jobs to bring in more money. Others have trouble finding any jobs at all.

Americans work in a wide range of jobs. Many city-dwellers work in offices, factories, schools, stores, and restaurants. Others build roads, houses, and other structures. Many rural people work at the same kinds of jobs as city-dwellers. Other rural people work in farming, mining, logging, fishing, and other occupations.

W. Wayne Lockwood/Corbis

OREGON
• Condon

MAINE
• Burntcoat Harbor

TEXAS

☆ Washington D.C.

Harvesting
Wheat
Near
Condon,
Oregon

Cowboy Barbecue At The Y.O. Ranch, Kerrville, Texas

CALIFORNIA
• Los Angeles

TEXAS
Kerrville •

LOUISIANA
• New Orleans

MASSACHUSETTS ☆ Boston

Food

Sometimes people say something is "as American as apple pie." Apple pie isn't the only well-known American food! Other favorites, such as hamburgers and hot dogs, are known all over the world. Some foods are associated with one part of America—such as Boston Baked Beans, New York bagels, New Orleans' spicy Cajun food, and Texas chili and Tex-Mex food. Many grocery stores and restaurants now sell these regional foods throughout the whole country.

Native Americans grew three well-known foods—corn, beans, and squash—long before Europeans arrived. Later immigrants brought new foods and cooking styles from their native countries. Many American restaurants specialize in Chinese, Thai, Mexican, Italian, or other cooking styles from other lands. But many of these foods have been changed to meet American tastes. People think of *chop suey* as a Chinese food, but it is actually Chinese-American, invented in the United States.

Cajun, Jambalaya, From New Orleans, Louisiana

Owen Franken/Corbis

Crock of Boston Baked Beans

DURGIN PARK BOSTON, MA U.S.A.

Dave Bartuff/Corbis

Sashimi From A Japanese Restaurant In Los Angeles, California

Nik Wheeler/Corbis

Pastimes

Americans enjoy a variety of pastimes. Some people spend their spare time quietly, watching television, reading, or playing video or other games. Many people enjoy sports such as baseball, football, basketball, hockey, soccer, and volleyball. Other favorite outdoor activities include riding bicycles, skating, hiking, camping, boating, hunting, fishing, and skiing.

Americans love going to movies, the theater, museums, and concerts. Shopping is popular, too! Shopping malls, stores, and garage sales are often full of busy shoppers. Many Americans also have hobbies such as painting or drawing, playing music, making crafts, or collecting things.

Outdoor Concert At Sand Harbor State Park, Nevada

Galen Rowell/Corbis

Video Game Players At Museum In Norfolk, Virginia

Richard T. Nowitz/Corbis

Cycling And Rollerblading On Muscle Beach In Venice, California

Patrick Ward/Corbis

Karl Weatherly/Corbis

CALIFORNIA
Lake Tahoe
Sand Harbor State Park
NEVADA
Venice
VIRGINIA
Norfolk

Skiing Above Lake Tahoe In California

Christmas At Universal Studios In Orlando, Florida

Issaquah
WASHINGTON
NEW YORK
Liberty Island
Grand Canyon National Park
ARIZONA
☆Atlanta
GEORGIA
Orlando•
FLORIDA

Kelly-Mooney Photography/Corbis

Holidays

Statue Of Liberty On Independence Day, Liberty Island, New York

Bill Ross/Corbis

Americans celebrate a number of religious and other holidays. Popular religious holidays include Easter, Christmas, and Hanukkah. Official holidays include President's Day, Martin Luther King Day, Memorial Day, Independence Day, and Labor Day. Other popular celebrations are New Year's Eve, New Year's Day, Valentine's Day, and Halloween.

The United States has been called "the land of the free" and "the land of opportunity." Many of its people have indeed been able to make better lives for themselves. Others have not been so fortunate. One of America's strengths—its variety of people—has also led to some problems. It is not easy to get so many people, from so many different backgrounds, to work together! But many people are working hard to make sure the United States continues to prosper and grow.

Coloring Easter Eggs In Issaquah, Washington

Philip James Corwin/Corbis

Reverend Martin Luther King, Jr., Atlanta, Georgia (1964)

Flip Schulke/Corbis

Sunset
On The
Grand
Canyon
National Park
In Arizona

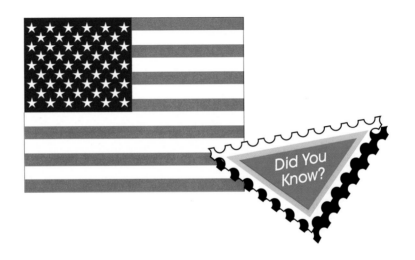

Today, the United States has about 2 million Native Americans. They are descended from the Eskimos and American Indians who lived in North America long before Columbus arrived.

Over 30 million Americans are African-Americans. Most of them descended from slaves that were freed in 1863.

Well over 20 million Americans are Hispanic people. They trace their roots to Spanish-speaking countries such as Mexico, Cuba, and other Central and South American nations.

Each year, almost 50 million tourists from other countries visit the United States. Many of them tour major cities and national parks.

The United States has almost 4 million miles of roads! Straightened out and laid end to end, they would circle the world 160 times.

The largest state is Alaska, and the smallest state is Rhode Island. Alaska is 483 times the size of Rhode Island!

California has over 30 million people—more than any other state. California even has more people than some countries.

Hawaii's islands are actually the tips of volcanoes built up from the floor of the ocean. Tourists often go to look at hot, melted rock still flowing from some Hawaiian volcanoes.

Glossary

coastal plain (KOAS–stull PLANE)
A coastal plain is fairly flat land that lies along a seacoast. Many Americans live on the coastal plain of the East Coast.

colonies (KOLL–uh–neez)
Colonies are regions ruled by far-away nations. The 13 colonies that first formed the United States were ruled by the king of England.

continents (KON–tih–nents)
Continents are large land areas that are mostly surrounded by oceans. The United States lies on the continent of North America.

desert (DEH–zert)
A desert is a very dry region that gets little rainfall. The southwestern United States has many desert areas.

immigrants (IH–mih–grents)
Immigrants are people who move to one land from another. Immigrants have come to the United States from all over the world.

prairies (PRAYR–eez)
Prairies are large grasslands. The Great Plains of the central United States were once covered with prairies.

rural (RUHR–ull)
Rural means "in the country." About one-quarter of America's people live in rural areas.

slavery (SLAY–ver–ee)
Slavery is "owning" another person. Before slavery was outlawed in 1863, many Africans were captured and brought to the United States as slaves.

suburbs (SUH–burbz)
Suburbs are smaller communities that lie close to cities. America's suburbs are growing rapidly.

tundra (TUN–druh)
The short grasslands of cold, harsh northern regions are called the tundra. Tundra regions are too cold to support trees or larger plants.

urban (UR–ben)
Urban means "in the city." About three-quarters of America's people live in or near urban areas.

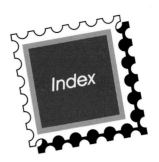

Index

A NATION DIVIDED
The Civil War Begins

American History Archives™

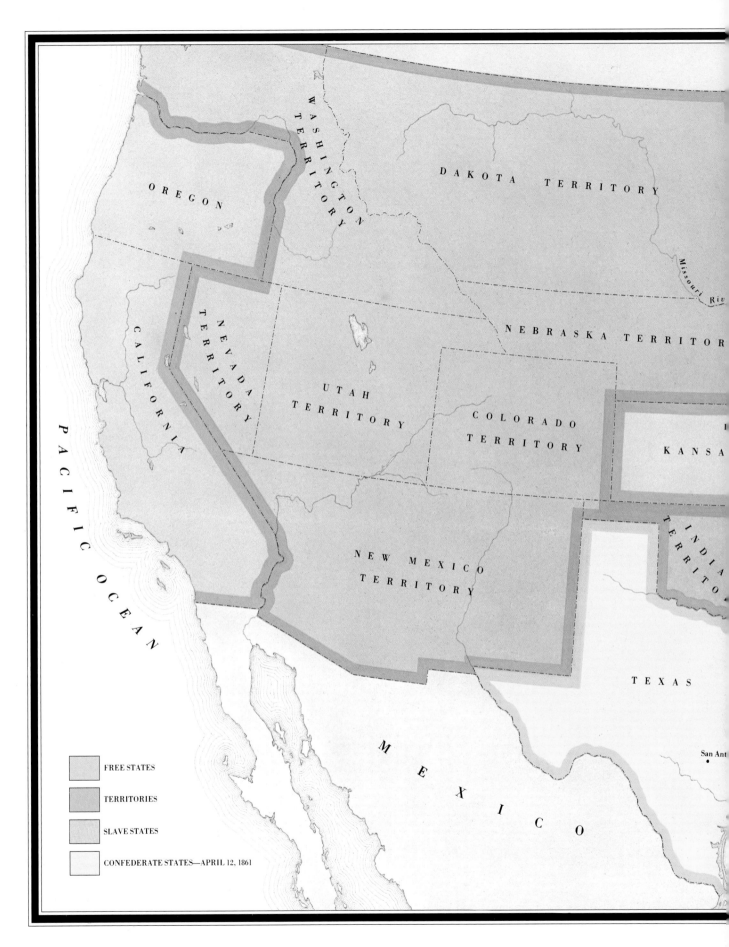

PACIFIC OCEAN

OREGON

WASHINGTON TERRITORY

DAKOTA TERRITORY

NEBRASKA TERRITOR

CALIFORNIA

NEVADA TERRITORY

UTAH TERRITORY

COLORADO TERRITORY

KANSA

Missouri Riv

INDIA
TERRITO

NEW MEXICO TERRITORY

TEXAS

MEXICO

San Ant

FREE STATES

TERRITORIES

SLAVE STATES

CONFEDERATE STATES—APRIL 12, 1861

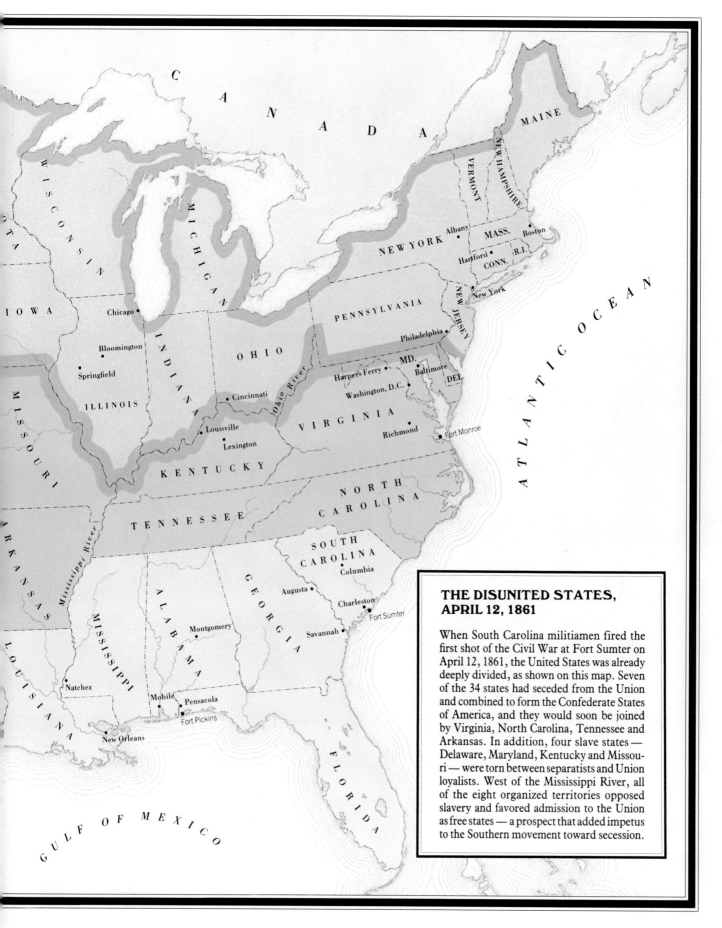

THE DISUNITED STATES, APRIL 12, 1861

When South Carolina militiamen fired the first shot of the Civil War at Fort Sumter on April 12, 1861, the United States was already deeply divided, as shown on this map. Seven of the 34 states had seceded from the Union and combined to form the Confederate States of America, and they would soon be joined by Virginia, North Carolina, Tennessee and Arkansas. In addition, four slave states — Delaware, Maryland, Kentucky and Missouri — were torn between separatists and Union loyalists. West of the Mississippi River, all of the eight organized territories opposed slavery and favored admission to the Union as free states — a prospect that added impetus to the Southern movement toward secession.

A NATION DIVIDED
The Civil War Begins

American History Archives™

Tom Carpenter
Creative Director

Heather Koshiol
Managing Editor

Julie Cisler, Shari Gross
Cover Design & Production

1 2 3 4 5 6 7 8 9 10 / 07 06 05 04 03

ISBN 1-58159-201-9

The History Channel Club
c/o North American Membership Group
12301 Whitewater Drive
Minnetonka, MN 55343
www.thehistorychannelclub.com

The Cover: Two young Americans, now enemy soldiers fighting for the Union (*left*) and the Confederacy, stand stiffly for portraits taken early in the Civil War. This was the first war to be covered in detail by the camera, and the soldiers sent many pictures home as mementos.

Published by North American Membership Group under license from Oxmoor House, Inc.

© 2003 Oxmoor House, Inc.

The Civil War
Editor: Gerald Simons
Designer: Herbert H. Quarmby
Chief Researcher: Jane Edwin

Editorial Staff for *A Nation Divided: The Civil War Begins* (originally published as *Brother against Brother*)
Associate Editors: Henry Woodhead (text); Richard Kenin (pictures)
Staff Writers: Adrienne George, C. Tyler Mathisen, John Newton, Kirk Y. Saunders
Researchers: Harris J. Andrews, Sara Schneidman (principals); Betsy Friedberg, Brian C. Pohanka, Alfreda Robertson, Jayne Wise
Assistant Designer: Jeanne Potter
Copy Coordinators: Allan Fallow, Victoria Lee, Brian Miller
Picture Coordinators: Rebecca Christoffersen, Eric Godwin
Editorial Assistant: Annette T. Wilkerson
Special Contributor: Peter Chaitin

Correspondents: Elisabeth Kraemer-Singh (Bonn); Maria Vincenza Aloisi (Paris); Ann Natanson (Rome).
Valuable assistance was also provided by: Gail Cameron Wescott (Atlanta); Juliette Tomlinson (Boston); Cheryl Crooks (Los Angeles); Cronin Buck Sleeper (Manchester Center, Vermont); Lynne Bachleda (Nashville); Carolyn Chubet (New York); Enid Farmer (Trevett, Maine).

The editors also thank the following individuals who gathered picture material for the Civil War series: Marion F. Briggs, Esther Brumberg, Diane Cook, Rosemary George, Catherine Gregory, Robin Raffer, Mariana Tait.

The Author:
William C. Davis was for 13 years editor of the Civil War Times Illustrated and is the author or editor of more than a dozen books on the Civil War, among them *Battle at Bull Run, The Orphan Brigade* and *The Deep Waters of the Proud*, the first in a three-volume narrative of the War. He is also editor of the six-volume photographic history of the conflict, *The Image of War: 1861-1865.*

The Consultants:
Colonel John R. Elting, USA (Ret.), a former Associate Professor at West Point, is the author of *Battles for Scandinavia* in the Time-Life Books World War II series and *The Battle of Bunker's Hill, The Battles of Saratoga, Military History and Atlas of the Napoleonic Wars* and *American Army Life.* He is also editor of the three volumes of *Military Uniforms in America, 1755-1867,* and associate editor of *The West Point Atlas of American Wars.*

James I. Robertson Jr., is C.P. Miles Professor of History at Virginia Tech. The recipient of the Nevins-Freeman Award and other prizes in the field of Civil War history, he has written or edited some 20 books, which include *The Stonewall Brigade, Civil War Books: A Critical Bibliography* and *Civil War Sites in Virginia.*

William A. Frassanito, a Civil War historian and lecturer specializing in photograph analysis, is the author of two award-winning studies, *Gettysburg: A Journey in Time* and *Antietam: The Photographic Legacy of America's Bloodiest Day.* He has also served as chief consultant to the photographic history series *The Image of War: 1861-1865.*

Les Jensen, Curator of the U.S. Army Transportation Museum at Fort Eustis, Virginia, specializes in Civil War artifacts and is a conservator of historic flags. He is a contributor to *The Image of War* series, a freelance writer and consultant for numerous Civil War publications and museums, and a member of the Company of Military Historians. He was formerly Curator of the Museum of the Confederacy in Richmond, Virginia.

Michael McAfee specializes in military uniforms and has been Curator of Uniforms and History at the West Point Museum since 1970. A fellow of the Company of Military Historians, he coedited with Colonel Elting *Long Endure: The Civil War Years,* and he collaborated with Frederick Todd on *American Military Equipage, 1851-1872.* He has written numerous articles for *Military Images Magazine,* as well as *Artillery of the American Revolution, 1775-1783.*

James P. Shenton, Professor of History at Columbia University, is a specialist in 19th Century American political and social history, with particular emphasis on the Civil War period. He is the author of *Robert John Walker* and *Reconstruction South.*

CONTENTS

Smoke-belching steamboats dock at the New Orleans levee at the mouth of the Mississippi. The mighty river bound North and South in mutually beneficial trad

The Two Americas

"It is no more possible for this country to pause in its career than for the free and untrammeled eagle to cease to soar," exulted Florida Congressman Stephen R. Mallory in 1859. And he had plenty of reason for optimism.

The decade of the 1850s brought the United States exceptional growth and prosperity. The population increased by 35 per cent, to more than 31 million. Railroad trackage more than trebled, reaching 30,000 miles. The production of all kinds of foodstuffs and manufactured goods rose dramatically. And the country had enormous resources to sustain its phenomenal progress: vast unoccupied lands, a network of navigable rivers, incalculable riches in timber, iron, coal, copper, California gold.

It was true that the 1850s also exacerbated the political tensions between North and South. But in the cold light of economics, the sections were interdependent—perhaps inseparable. Southern plantations provided bountiful raw materials for the industrial North, and Northern factories made most of the finished goods consumed by the South. "In brief and in short," concluded Senator Thomas Hart Benton of Missouri, "the two halves of this Union were made for each other as much as Adam and Eve."

Boom Time in the Cotton Kingdom

The famed Southern boast that "Cotton is king!" became increasingly true in the 1850s. Though many plantations thrived on rice, tobacco and other cash crops, more and more land was planted in cotton to meet the demands of British and Yankee textile mills, and more and more slaves were put to work bringing in the harvests. The annual yield soared from two million bales in 1849 to 5.7 million bales in 1859. This amounted to seven eighths of the world's cotton and more than half of all American exports.

Slaves pick cotton while o[...] process the harvest in a cotton gi[...] stacks exhaling smoke at rear. [...] cotton was planted in spring and [...] summer; the picking, ginning, b[...] and shipping lasted into early wi[...]

A workaday plantation comprises a big house *(center)* flanked by slave quarters, smokehouses, gardens and stockyards. Large plantations were virtually self-sufficient.

Laboring alongside hired whites, a gang of slaves harvests rice under a planter's direction. A planter would consider it a good year if each field slave produced a profit of $250.

The Lordly Life of the Landed Gentry

The popular notion of life in the South was set by a small minority, the well-to-do planters. They liked to think of themselves as heirs to the traditions of the knights and cavaliers, and they played the part stylishly, practicing chivalry toward women, kindness to inferiors and an elaborate code of honor among equals. The planters cultivated a taste for blooded horses, fine foxhounds, handmade firearms, and Southern belles of affluent families. And many studied the arts of war. A Mississippi planter, Jefferson Davis, said with pride that only in the South did "gentlemen go to a military academy who do not intend to follow the profession of arms."

Spectators head toward the Oakland House and Race Course in Louisville, Kentucky. Planters, by and large, were keen judges of horseflesh and inveterate bettors. Some brought surplus slaves to the races to back especially large bets.

Wealthy Virginians gather at a river for a mass baptism. Virginia's Tidewater planters tended to be Episcopalians. According to an old local saying, there were many ways to go to heaven, but a gentleman would choose the Episcopalian way.

A plantation owner on horseback holds his gun at the ready while his dogs attack a stag. Southern men, rich and poor alike, learned to ride and shoot in early boyhood.

Southern belles ascend a grand staircase while their beaux wait at the foot. Lavish house parties and balls were held frequently by wealthy planters. "The Northerner loves to make money," noted a Mississippian, "the Southerner to spend it."

Huntsville, Alabama, has a rural look in this view, painted around 1850. "From the quiet appearance of their towns," said a visiting Yankee, "the stranger would think business was taking a siesta."

A Realm of Sleepy Towns and Scattered Hamlets

"Every step one takes in the South," wrote a British visitor in 1856, "one is struck with the rough look of the whole civilization. Towns and villages are few and far between." Cities were scarcer still, and practically all of them were relatively small; Charleston, Richmond and Savannah each had populations of less than 40,000. Only New Orleans, with about 150,000 inhabitants, was comparable to Northern cities in size and diversity.

The bucolic landscape and the slow, agrarian life were just what most Southerners desired. Said an Alabama politician: "We want no manufactures; we desire no trading, no mechanical or manufacturing classes. As long as we have our rice, our sugar, our tobacco and our cotton, we can command wealth to purchase all we want."

In Athens, Georgia, the buildings of Franklin College (later the University of Georgia) stand atop a wooded hill (left) across the Oconee River from the terminus of the Georgia Railway. Though Athens was founded in 1801, it had only 3,848 inhabitants by 1860.

Melting Pots for New Americans

In marked contrast to their Southern counterparts, Northern cities were crowded, bustling, boisterous places, many expanding too fast to digest their growth. The population of New York soared from 515,000 to 814,000 in the 1850s. Chicago, incorporated as a city in 1837 with a population of 4,170, had 112,000 inhabitants in 1860.

Foreign voices were heard on all sides. Between 1850 and 1860, more than 2.8 million immigrants poured into port cities; nearly one half of the New York population was foreign-born. Most of the immigrants drudged long hours for meager pay and lived in squalor. But they adapted readily to their new country, embraced its egalitarian values and made great strides as Americans. By the 1850s, the Irish had become political powers in Boston, Philadelphia and New York, and the Germans were the dominant voting bloc in St. Louis and Milwaukee.

Many Americans resented the foreign influx, but others exulted in it. "We are not a narrow tribe of men whose blood has been debased by maintaining an exclusive succession among ourselves," wrote novelist Herman Melville. "No: our blood is as the flood of the Amazon, made up of a thousand noble currents all pouring into one."

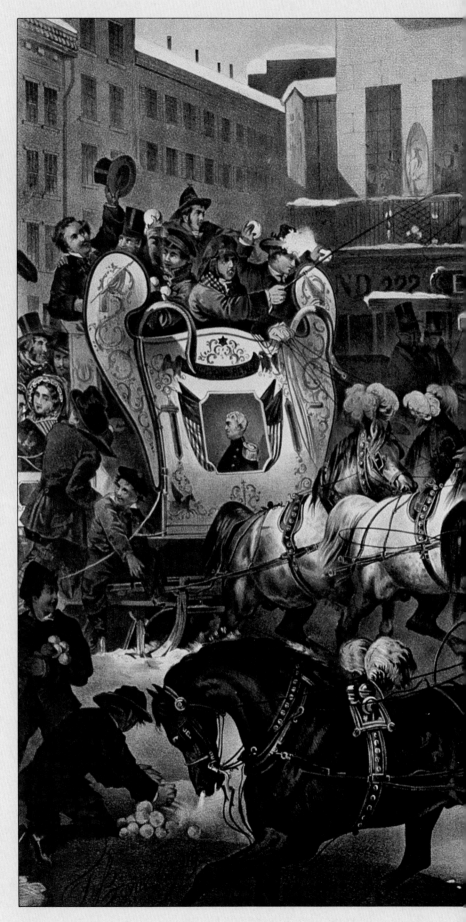

A wild snowball fight among rowdy New Yorkers disrupts traffic in front of P. T. Barnum's curiosity museum in lower Manhattan in 1855. Rivalries between neighborhoods, ethnic groups and political clubs often led to pitched battles in the streets.

16

The North's "Great, Silent Revolution"

Throughout the 1850s, the North industrialized at almost breakneck speed. By the close of the decade, the Northern states contained four fifths of America's factories, two thirds of the nation's railroad mileage and practically all of its shipyards. The New York *Tribune* described the economic development of the North as "a great, silent revolution."

But the revolution was not really noiseless at all. It thrived on clattering, roaring phalanxes of new machines: circular saws, power looms, rotary presses, hydraulic turbines, shoe peggers, sewing machines, steam locomotives, corn planters, wheat drills, reapers, road scrapers, posthole augers. These inventions and countless others made "Yankee ingenuity" an international byword, and when Samuel Colt of Connecticut perfected the use of standardized, mass-produced, interchangeable components for his revolver, the British dubbed his method of manufacturing "the American system."

Workers fashion railroad forgings at a rolling mill in New Jersey. In the railroad craze of the 1850s, a number of lines went broke by overbuilding or engaging in rate-cutting wars.

Factories in Pittsburgh spew clouds of smoke in this 1838 painting. Pittsburgh owed its success to an enormous vein of bituminous coal that ran beneath the city and to iron-ore deposits nearby.

Standing in the bow of a bobbing boat, a Yankee harpooner prepares to deliver the death blow to a foundering whale. In the 1850s, when whaling was at its peak, more than 700 New England-based ships ranged the globe, bringing home catches worth an average of eight million dollars a year.

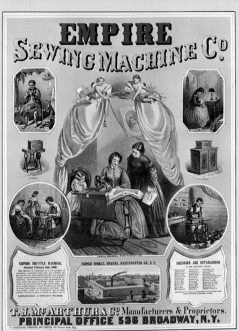

A sewing-machine advertisement features improved models for the home and workshop. By 1859, Northern factories were turning out 37,000 machines a year.

Yankee families socialize while making maple sugar *(top)* and apple cider *(detail, bottom)*. Such farm products were moved rapidly to urban markets on New England's extensive transportation system.

Living By a Gospel of Hard Work

Northern prosperity was deeply grounded in the Protestant work ethic. Ministers and itinerant evangelists preached a gospel of hard work, thrift and self-discipline. Worldly success was interpreted as a sign of God's favor, but labor was considered to be an end in itself rather than merely a means to an end.

Nowhere was this austere creed practiced more faithfully than on the many small farms of New England, where families produced a great variety of vegetables, fruit, poultry and dairy goods. Here the work ethic fostered excellence. "Fifty acres properly managed," wrote a progressive Yankee, "will produce more than 500 badly conducted."

An evangelist exhorts a swooning crowd at a revival meeting. Preachers at such gatherings painted grim word pictures of the evils of drink. Partly as a result, the per capita intake of alcohol dropped and the productivity of labor rose sharply.

Neighboring Yankee farmers join forces to harvest a crop of hay along the shores of the Acushnet River in southeastern Massachusetts.

Pride and Peril in the "Wisest System Ever Devised"

When Andrew Jackson described Americans as "guardians of freedom for the human race," and when James K. Polk spoke of American government as "this most admirable and wisest system ever devised," the Presidents' sentiments were not considered hyperbolic by the vast majority of their countrymen. To Northerners and Southerners alike, such statements represented the truth, pure and simple.

Besides their abiding faith in democratic ideals, Americans everywhere shared an avid interest in the political process that translated those ideals into practice. Patriotic celebrations on the Fourth of July and Washington's Birthday were built around political speeches, and during the rest of the year any candidate appealing for votes could count on drawing a fair-sized crowd. Indeed, electioneering appeared to be a great constant in American life. The visiting English novelist Charles Dickens remarked: "Directly that the acrimony of the last election is over, the acrimony of the next begins."

American politics was a fiercely partisan affair, and for decades, that had been all to the good, spurring the people's interest in national issues, putting new ideas and policies to the test of the ballot box. But as the 1850s drew to a close, thoughtful citizens wondered whether their shared ideals could sustain the nation through its mounting crises—or whether their political passions would split the Union.

Verdict of the People, painted by noted American artist George Caleb Bingham, shows a street scene in a Missouri town as the results of an election are announced. The facial expressions of the listeners clearly indicate whether their candidate was the winner or the loser.

One Nation, Divisible

"The Southern people, driven to the wall, have no remedy but that of political independence. Forbearance has not only ceased to be a virtue, but has become absolute cowardice."

NEW ORLEANS *DAILY CRESCENT*, DECEMBER 17, 1860

1

Nothing could keep Edmund Ruffin away from the secession convention. Not his grief for his dear daughter Elizabeth, who had just died in childbirth. Not the heavy storm that had covered his plantation north of Richmond, Virginia, with nine inches of snow and was discommoding travelers in the region. Ruffin had long been agitating for Southern independence, and now that South Carolina was on the verge of quitting the United States, he was determined to be there, to witness with his own dimming eyes (he was 66) the dawn of the glorious new era. So on December 17, 1860, the old man packed his luggage, journeyed by carriage and river steamer to Richmond, and there caught a southbound train.

Ruffin's destination was the South Carolina capital, Columbia, where delegates from all over the state convened on the 17th for the declared purpose of terminating relations with the government "known as the United States of America." But during a stop along the way at Wilmington, North Carolina, Ruffin learned that the convention had been driven out of Columbia by an outbreak of smallpox and had reconvened in Charleston—an appropriate move, since that city had always been a hotbed of secessionist sentiment. He changed trains accordingly and arrived in Charleston on the morning of December 19. He was lucky to find accommodation in a tiny, unheated room in the Charleston Hotel.

The town was overflowing with enthusiastic Southern patriots—Southrons, they called themselves. In addition to the convention delegates, the entire South Carolina government was on hand, along with such visiting dignitaries as the Governor of Florida, official representatives of Alabama and Mississippi, four former United States senators and one former United States attorney general. Ruffin encountered scores of old friends and fellow "fire-eaters" who had been leaders in the fight to break up the Union. They were the gentry of the South: planters and newspaper publishers, judges and lawyers, clergymen and bankers—some of them wearing the bright uniforms and the gold braid of officers in the militia. David F. Jamison, a gentleman-scholar who lived quite graciously on the proceeds of a 2,000-acre, 70-slave plantation, was the presiding officer of the convention, and he saw to it that Ruffin would have a seat in the two jam-packed convention buildings.

Using a gavel incised with the word "Secession," President Jamison called the session of December 19 to order in St. Andrew's Hall, a small auditorium where speakers could make themselves heard more easily than in the big auditorium of Institute Hall. The exact language of the Ordinance of Secession was still being mooted in committee, and Jamison pointedly read a telegram from the Governor of Alabama urging the convention to brook no delay.

Many things remained to be settled. Concurrent with secession, the state of South

24

Cockades of South Carolina palmetto fronds were worn by Charlestonians to symbolize their defiance of the Union at the secession convention in December of 1860. Later, the cockades were worn throughout the South as emblems of sectional solidarity.

Carolina would cease to be bound by federal law, and a complete new code for the infant republic of South Carolina would have to be framed. Local patriots had to be appointed to take over the functions of United States officials. How best could the postal service be handled? What regulations would need to be adopted for collecting customs at the port of Charleston?

The delegates quickly addressed themselves to one matter that soon would become a critical problem. A committee was appointed to report on United States properties inside the territorial limits of South Carolina; most prominent of these were three federal military installations in Charleston Harbor —Fort Moultrie, Castle Pinckney and Fort Sumter. A resolution was then passed instructing the Committee on Foreign Relations to send three commissioners to Washington to negotiate with the United States government for the transfer of all such real estate to the new republic of South Carolina. Regarding this and other momentous issues, Edmund Ruffin made a laconic entry in his diary: "Heard several interesting discussions on subjects incidental and preliminary to the act of secession."

Everyone was disappointed when the day ended without a formal declaration of secession. But during the delay, the symbols of rebellion—the colors and devices of South Carolina—had time to come into full bloom throughout Charleston. Assistant Surgeon Samuel Crawford, attached to the small federal garrison at Fort Moultrie, reported that "blue cockades and cockades of palmetto appeared in every hat; flags of all description, except the National colors, were everywhere displayed. The enthusiasm spread to more practical walks of trade, and the busi-

ness streets were gay with bunting and flags, as the tradespeople, many of whom were Northern men, commended themselves to the popular clamor."

At noon the next day in St. Andrew's Hall, Ruffin attended a closed meeting of the Committee to Prepare an Ordinance of Secession. The product of the committeemen's anxious travail was read aloud:

We, the people of the State of South Carolina, in Convention assembled, do declare and ordain . . . that the union now subsisting between South Carolina and other States under the name of "The United States of America" is hereby dissolved.

At 1:15 p.m. all 169 delegates voted to adopt the ordinance as read. The document was then turned over to the attorney general of South Carolina to see that it was properly engrossed. The public signing ceremony was scheduled to take place in Institute Hall at 7 o'clock that evening.

The delegates—the founding fathers of the new nation—emerged from the hall and were immediately greeted by the start of a long, loud, citywide celebration. Church bells were rung, cannon were fired and joy was nearly universal. One of the few people to admit dissatisfaction was a cranky old judge named James Louis Petigru. Petigru was walking down Broad Street when the bell ringing began and, upon bumping into a friend at the city hall, he inquired sourly of the man, "Where's the fire?" Petigru's friend replied that there was no fire, just happy noise to celebrate secession. "I tell you there is a fire," the judge retorted. "They have this day set a blazing torch to the temple of Constitutional liberty and, please

Host to the South Carolina secession convention, the city of Charleston spreads outward along Meeting Street in this prewar photograph taken from the steeple of St. Michael's Church. The tall façade of the Mills House, hotel headquarters for the secession dignitaries, rises beyond the big tree at left. The city hall appears at bottom right.

A throng of cheering Southern separatists rallies in front of Charleston's Mills House during the South Carolina secession crisis of December 1860. Impassioned speakers on the hotel balcony kept whipping up the crowd's enthusiasm.

God, we shall have no more peace forever."

At 7 p.m., the delegates to the convention marched into Institute Hall through dense crowds of celebrants. The signing ceremony took two hours. Finally, President Jamison held up the completed document and declared, "I proclaim the State of South Carolina an independent commonwealth." An enormous roar of approval shook the hall. The deed had been done.

The convention adjourned, and old Edmund Ruffin—honored with the gift of a pen that had signed the Ordinance of Secession—made his way back to the Charleston Hotel. Once he had reached his room, he took out his diary and contentedly summed up the hectic scene: "Military companies paraded, salutes were fired, and as night came on, bonfires, made of barrels of rosin, were lighted in the principal streets, rockets discharged and innumerable crackers discharged by the boys. As I now write, after 10 p.m., I hear the distant sound of rejoicing, with music of a military band, as if there were no thought of ceasing."

Exactly what had happened in Charleston on December 20, 1860? The answer was by no means certain at the time.

According to Northerners with a Consti-

A special edition of the Charleston *Mercury* hails South Carolina's vote to secede. The extra hit the streets at 1:30 p.m. on December 20, 1860, just 15 minutes after the Ordinance of Secession was passed.

tutional turn of mind, nothing had happened; the United States was a sovereign nation, not a mere confederation of independent states; thus by its very nature the republic was indivisible, and secession was impossible. Other, more pragmatic Northerners regarded secession as a very real crime against the Constitution, a breach of popular contract so grave that force of arms would have to put it right. Most Southerners, for their part, were willing to take up arms to defend their action. And many people on both sides saw secession as the only peaceful way out of their quarrels.

In any case, the first of the Southern states had seceded. It was the beginning of the end of the early Union—an event that Southerners called the second American Revolution. Looked at another way, it marked the end of the beginning—an abrupt halt to the nation's first phase of helter-skelter growth. It would lead, after four months of increasing tension and hostility, to the start of the deadliest of American wars, a four-year struggle that would consume the lives of more than 620,000 young Americans, or roughly one out of every 50 citizens.

That the nation was so vigorous made its breakup and descent into war all the more tragic. Europeans were beginning to recognize the United States as a world power and the epitome of democratic ideals. Indications of prosperity and progress were abundant: Well-off families in large cities were beginning to have indoor privies; plans were in the works for a railroad to California; and a transatlantic cable—which had twice barely failed—seemed certain to succeed in the near future. Moreover, some gifted leaders had strode the political stage in recent decades—men who had fashioned careful com-

CHARLESTON
MERCURY
EXTRA:

Passed unanimously at 1.15 o'clock, P. M. December 20th, 1860.

AN ORDINANCE

To dissolve the Union between the State of South Carolina and other States united with her under the compact entitled " The Constitution of the United States of America."

We, the People of the State of South Carolina, in Convention assembled, do declare and ordain, and it is hereby declared and ordained,

That the Ordinance adopted by us in Convention, on the twenty-third day of May, in the year of our Lord one thousand seven hundred and eighty-eight, whereby the Constitution of the United States of America was ratified, and also, all Acts and parts of Acts of the General Assembly of this State, ratifying amendments of the said Constitution, are hereby repealed; and that the union now subsisting between South Carolina and other States, under the name of "The United States of America," is hereby dissolved.

THE
UNION
IS
DISSOLVED!

neurs moved steadily inland along the rivers, building mills and factories to exploit the ample water power. They were followed by plenty of surplus workers from the coastal cities. By the early years of the 19th Century, the North was becoming a region of large-scale industry, big cities and long-distance commerce, with a great deal of small-scale farming of varied food crops.

In the South, the terrain and climate favored an agrarian way of life. Good land was plentiful and accessible, for the coastal plain extended well inland, and the rivers were navigable to the fall line far to the west. The warm weather, the long growing seasons and the great stretches of level, unbroken terrain were just right for the plantation system—a method of large-scale, intensive farming in which gangs of unskilled laborers worked to cultivate a single cash crop: tobacco or rice, sugar cane or long-staple cotton. The South's most important crop, short-staple cotton, became profitable in the 1790s, when Eli Whitney's cotton gin solved the problem of separating the tough seeds from the fleecy white fiber.

At first, workers were everywhere in short supply in the Southern colonies, with white indentured servants doing much of the menial labor. But the real plantation work forces were gradually provided by the slave trade with Africa and the West Indies. In the 17th Century, slavery was still widely regarded as a legitimate means of maintaining the subservience of conquered enemies or analphabetic inferiors. More than a century later, slaves were recognized as a form of property in the United States Constitution. Being mere chattel, the slaves were not citizens and had no vote. But in an effort to redress the imbalance of national representa-

promises to resolve sectional disputes. But the plain fact of the matter was that the North and the South had become so different—so damnably incompatible and antagonistic—that no amount of political ingenuity could avail.

The two sections had been following divergent paths ever since the start of settlement in America. Geography and climate at once began shaping radically different economic and social patterns in the North and in the South. In the upper Atlantic regions, the terrain was hilly and rocky, with the interior heavily forested and difficult of access. These conditions tended to keep farms small and to build up large pools of population along the coast; many Northern settlers became seamen, fishermen, shipbuilders and merchants. When the Industrial Revolution began late in the 18th Century, entrepre-

tion between the thinly settled South and the populous North, the Southern states were allowed to count each slave as three fifths of a person for their Congressional apportionment. Thus an added indignity for slaves: Votes conferred by the head count of blacks were cast by whites to keep the slaves servile.

As black slavery spread in the South during the 18th Century, opposition to it spread in the North. The first important protests came from austere Protestant groups, primarily the Quakers, who objected to the ownership of people on moral grounds. Oth-

er Northerners, however, considered such protests academic, for slavery was fading out in their states; manufacturers and businessmen preferred self-sufficient employees who could be hired and fired to suit economic conditions. Thus, since the Northern states did not need or want slaves, they outlawed slavery one by one.

There were enlightened Southern planters who agreed that slavery—they referred to it as "our peculiar domestic institution"—was distasteful. Some liberals among them began freeing their slaves. Other planters pointed

out correctly that they were far more humane than their South American counterparts, who tended to work their slaves to death. Still, the Southern planters profited handsomely by whatever degree of humane treatment they practiced. By 1808, when the United States became the last democratic nation to ban international slave trade, Southern slaves were living long enough, and reproducing fast enough, to provide their masters with a lucrative side line of salable human chattel.

It turned out that slavery and the plantation system were self-perpetuating. In a pattern set early in the tobacco plantations of Virginia, intensive one-crop farming quickly exhausted even the best of soils. The big planters, who lived like feudal lords on very small amounts of cash, declined to sacrifice profits by rotating crops, letting fields lie fallow, or fertilizing to any substantial degree. Instead, the planters purchased more and more land—and so they needed more and more slaves to work the new holdings. Latecomers established plantations farther to the west and south, practicing the same one-crop

ting shipment to mills in New
nd and Great Britain, bales of
n line a street near the New
ns docks in the 1850s. Although
outhern states produced most
world's cotton, they possessed
per cent of the nation's cotton-
facturing capability.

Tall-masted merchant ships crowd
the South Street docks in New
York City, the North's busiest port.
In the 1850s, America's merchant
marine replaced England's as
the leader in world commerce.

style of agriculture, usually with cotton.

By the early 18th Century, the great Virginia families with plantations dotting the Tidewater were expanding inland, driving the South's small yeoman farmers ahead of them into less favorable lands in the piedmont areas and the Appalachians beyond. By the 1820s, cotton culture was spreading rapidly southward into the Gulf Coast regions, and during the next decade it overleaped the Mississippi into Texas.

Production of cotton rose steeply—from $15 million in 1810 to $63 million in 1840. The value of slaves also increased sharply, from $600 each in 1810 to $1,000 in 1840 to $1,200 and even $1,800 for a prime field hand on the eve of secession. But the lot of the planters did not improve. Lacking middlemen and credit arrangements of their own, planters were victimized by Northern factors, who would pay only the prices set by the English market. Planters suffered cruelly from the volatile American economy, with its quick succession of booms and busts, flush times and depressions.

From time to time, constructive Southerners attempted to diversify their economy—to industrialize, if only to the extent of building mills to process their own cotton. But the Southern planters, slave-poor and land-poor in their struggle to expand apace with demand, had very little to invest; the entire South could not muster as much capital as the single state of New York. Moreover, Southern efforts to raise Yankee capital for building mills and factories generally failed; Northern bankers and financiers were unwilling to invest in a region that lacked both a free labor supply and an adequate transportation system.

In the view of many Southerners, the

EMIGRATION

UP THE MISSISSIPPI RIVER.

The attention of Emigrants and the Public generally, is called to the now rapidly improving

TERRITORY OF MINNESOTA,

Containing a population of 150,000, and goes into the Union as a State during the present year. According to an act of Congress passed last February, the State is munificently endowed with Lands for Public Schools and State Universities, also granting five per cent. on all sales of U. S. Lands for Internal Improvements. On the 3d March, 1857, grants of Land from Congress was made to the leading Trunk Railroads in Minnesota, so that in a short time the trip from New Orleans to any part of the State will be made in from two and a half to three days. The

CITY OF NININGER,

Situated on the Mississippi River, 35 miles below St. Paul, is now a prominent point for a large Commercial Town, being backed by an extensive Agricultural, Grazing and Farming Country ; has fine streams in the interior, well adapted for Milling in all its branches ; and Manufacturing **WATER POWER** to any extent.

Mr. JOHN NININGER, (a Gentleman of large means, ideas and liberality, speaking the various languages,) is the principal Proprietor of **Nininger**. He laid it out on such principles as to encourage all **MECHANICS**, Merchants, or Professions of all kinds, on the same equality and footing ; the consequence is, the place has gone ahead with such rapidity that it is now an established City, and will annually double in population for years to come.

Persons arriving by Ship or otherwise, can be transferred without expense to Steamers going to Saint Louis ; or stop at Cairo, and take Railroad to Dunleith (on the Mississippi). Steamboats leave Saint Louis and Dunleith daily for **NININGER**, and make the trip from Dunleith in 36 to 48 hours.

NOTICES.

1. All Railroads and Steamboats giving this card a conspicuous place, or gratuitous insertion in their cards. AIDS THE EMIGRANT and forwards their own interest.

2. For authentic documents, reliable information, and all particulars in regard to Occupations, Wages, Pre-empting Lands in neighborhood, Lumber, Price of Lots, Expenses, &c., apply to

THOMAS B. WINSTON, 27 Camp street, New Orleans.
ROBERT CAMPBELL, St. Louis.
JOSEPH B. FORBES, Dunleith.

South had become a hapless colonial region that was exploited by the industrialized North. "Financially we are more enslaved than our Negroes," complained an Alabamian. In 1851 a newspaper in Alabama published a long and bitter inventory of the ways in which the South was a vassal to the North:

"We purchase all our luxuries and necessities from the North. Our slaves are clothed with Northern manufactured goods, have Northern hats and shoes, work with Northern hoes, plows and other implements. The slaveholder dresses in Northern goods, rides in a Northern saddle, sports his Northern carriage, reads Northern books. In Northern vessels his products are carried to market, his cotton is ginned with Northern gins, his sugar is crushed and preserved with Northern machinery, his rivers are navigated by Northern steamboats. His son is educated at a Northern college, his daughter receives the finishing polish at a Northern seminary; his doctor graduates at a Northern medical college, his schools are furnished with Northern teachers, and he is furnished with Northern inventions."

Against this backdrop of economic troubles, a succession of great political crises beset the nation in the first half of the 19th Century. All of them were brought to seemingly viable resolutions. But each one raised the level of sectional hostility to new heights, and each one left behind a legacy of deepening rancor and frustration. By the beginning of the decade of the 1850s, there was precious little left of the sense of common interest and mutual sympathy that had bound the North and the South together during the American Revolution.

It was the country's great good fortune in this period to be served by three giants—political leaders who represented different interests with power, clarity, honest conviction and unfailing responsibility. Daniel Webster of New Hampshire and later Massachusetts spoke for mercantile, antislavery New England. Henry Clay of Kentucky, representing both slaveowners and a strong antislavery element in his border state, became the mediator for the nation. John C. Calhoun of South Carolina captured in his changing political outlook the course of the country and the trend of the times: He began his career as an ardent nationalist and ended it as a passionate sectionalist.

Lawyer Calhoun cut an impressive figure when he arrived in Washington in 1811 as a newly elected Congressman from South Carolina. At the age of 29 he was tall and square-shouldered, a man with the burning eyes of a visionary. His seriousness of purpose and his Calvinist piety allowed little room for humor; logic and law were what consumed his thoughts. He was said to have sent his wife-to-be a love poem consisting of 12 lines, each of which started with the word "Whereas"—except for the last, which began with "Therefore."

In his calm, crisp courtroom manner, Calhoun swayed men and won votes with his own particular brand of radical patriotism. Declaring that "the honor of a nation is its life," he successfully pushed for war against British aggression in 1812. Later he joined with Henry Clay to promote what came to be called the "American system," a master plan for national strength and growth that included proposals for national defense, a national protective import tariff, a national bank for a uniform currency and a nationwide transportation system.

Calhoun's opponents, chiefly conservative

New Englanders, argued that the Constitution did not delegate such sweeping powers to the federal government, that the American system would usurp authority belonging to the individual states. But the notion of states' rights was anathema to young Calhoun. "We are under the most imperious obligation to counteract every tendency to disunion," he declared. "Let us, then, bind the Republic together with a perfect system of roads and canals. Let us conquer space."

On February 13, 1819, the first of the period's great struggles was joined. James Tallmadge, an obscure one-term Representative from New York, introduced a resolution that electrified the United States Congress. The debate that it provoked came, the aging Thomas Jefferson wrote, "like a firebell in the night," which "awakened me and filled me with terror. I considered it at once the knell of the union." To another former President, John Quincy Adams, it seemed to be "a title page to a great tragic volume."

Tallmadge's measure sought to prohibit slavery in the Missouri Territory, a section of the Louisiana Purchase that was petitioning to enter the Union as a slave state. The proposed restriction reflected a growing anti-slavery sentiment on the part of Northern legislators and represented a challenge that the South could ill afford to ignore, for it had implications that extended far beyond the status of Missouri. It was cotton that produced the lion's share of the South's income, and planters were fearful that unless the cultivation of cotton continued to expand, their whole economy would wither and die as cultivated areas were exhausted. And, just as frightening to Southerners, it threatened to shift the balance of power in Washington in favor of the North.

Daniel Webster of Massachusetts, whose noncommittal attitude toward slavery often prompted criticism, outraged abolitionists with his speech in favor of the 1850 Compromise condoning slavery. Poet Ralph Waldo Emerson accused him of venality in a bitter couplet: "Why did all manly gifts in Webster fail? / He wrote on Nature's grandest brow, *For Sale.*"

Kentucky's Henry Clay, whose Compromise of 1850 reconciled North and South for a decade, presented himself as a presidential candidate five times and was five times rebuffed. Out of his disappointments came his famous declaration that he "would rather be right than be President."

South Carolina's John C. Calh(right) was so unyielding anpassionate in his defense of Southrights that a visiting Englishcalled him both "the cast-iron mand "a volcano in full for

Southerners had already lost control of the House of Representatives to the Northern states, whose populations were swelling as immigration increased. The Senate was controlled by neither section: Of 22 states in the nation in 1819, exactly half were free and half were slave. But if Missouri entered the Union as a free state, the Senatorial balance would tip against slavery. The South would then be helpless to prevent the passage of ruinous legislation: tariffs that crippled the Southern cotton trade with Europe; huge funds allocated to the development of ports, canals and turnpikes beneficial to the North; eventually, the abolition of slavery, even in the slave states.

The volatile issue of the extension of slavery to Missouri touched off an acrimonious debate that spanned two sessions of Congress. The Northerners were seething with moral outrage. "How long will the desire for wealth render us blind to the sin of holding both the bodies and souls of our fellow men in chains?" demanded Representative Arthur Livermore of New Hampshire. "Do not, for the sake of cotton and tobacco, let it be told to future ages that, while pretending to love liberty, we have purchased an extensive country to disgrace it with the foulest reproach to nations!"

The Southern planters, trapped in their dependence on slavery, accused Northerners of exaggerating the evils of the institution and challenged the right of the North to meddle in the affairs of the South. "The slaveholding states," declared the Lexington, Kentucky, *Western Monitor*, "will not brook an invasion of their rights. They will not be driven by compulsion to the emancipation, even gradually, of their states."

Not until 1820 was the debate over the

admission of Missouri finally calmed by moderates. Henry Clay had stepped forward with a compromise that seemingly settled the slavery issue. To preserve the tenuous balance in the Senate, Missouri was to be admitted as a slave state and Maine would come into the Union as a free state. Further, a demarcation line would be drawn from east to west at latitude 36° 30'. Henceforth, all new states that might be fashioned from Louisiana Purchase territories north of that line would be free, whereas all of those below it would be slave.

The Missouri Compromise papered over the problem of the extension of slavery, but it was satisfactory to no one. For the first time in the short history of the nation, an action by Congress had aligned the states against each other on a sectional basis. Suspicions grew on both sides. Northerners suspected that a Southern cabal they called "the Slave Power" was conspiring to circumvent the principle of rule by the majority. Southerners, in turn, suspected that Northerners were plotting to destroy them. Said James M. Garnett of Virginia, "It would seem as if all the devils incarnate, both in the Eastern and Northern states, are in league against us."

Calhoun did his best to allay Southern fears of a Northern conspiracy against slavery. But cries for help from the planters of South Carolina were pulling him to their side. Tariffs that protected the profits of Northern manufacturers caused increasing hardship in the South, raising the prices that Southerners had to pay for imported manufactures. And then, in the 1820s, the Southern predicament was further exacerbated by a recession.

More and more Southerners, Calhoun in-

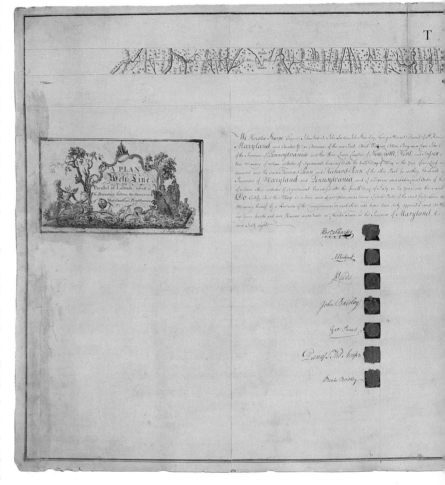

cluded, turned against nationalism. In 1827, while serving as Vice President in the administration of John Quincy Adams, he made his first break with his past. On the Senate floor, with the vote tied on a new tariff bill, Calhoun cast the decisive ballot against it. But the next year, rival politicians managed to force through Congress another, higher tariff on a variety of manufactured goods. Angry Southerners labeled it the Tariff of Abominations, and soon they were blaming it for all their economic ills.

In Calhoun's South Carolina, those troubles were acute. As plantation profits declined during the recession, planters aban-

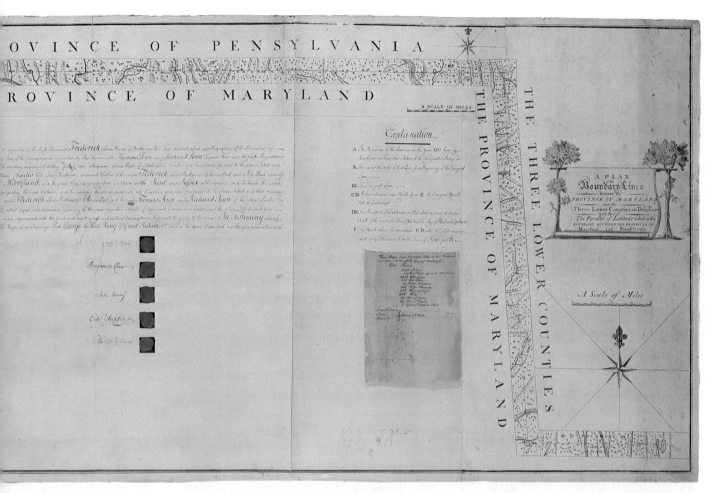

The Maryland-Pennsylvania boundary—the Mason-Dixon line—was established by Charles Mason and Jeremiah Dixon, who surveyed and mapped it in the 1760s to settle a border dispute. The boundary was accepted as the eastern end of the dividing line between slave and free states during arguments that led to the Missouri Compromise of 1820.

doned their fields. Roads and bridges fell into ruin. Calhoun wrote his brother-in-law in 1828: "Our staples hardly return the expense of cultivation, and land and Negroes have fallen to the lowest price and can scarcely be sold at the present depressed rates." A vocal group of South Carolina radicals went so far as to speak of secession as a means of eradicating the intolerable tax.

Calhoun now faced a dilemma. Elected to serve as Vice President under Andrew Jackson, he wanted to succeed to the presidency. But to stand any chance he would have to tread a precarious path, satisfying the radicals at home, maintaining Jackson's friend-

ship, and at the same time somehow moderating the angry reaction of the Northern businessmen who were in favor of protective tariffs. What he needed was a program.

In the summer of 1828, Calhoun had secluded himself at Fort Hill, his plantation in Pendleton District, to study American state papers in search of a defense against the tariff. He paid particular attention to the 1781 Articles of Confederation, which recognized the "sovereignty, freedom, and independence" of each state, and to the Kentucky and Virginia Resolutions of 1798 and 1799, which stated the controversial opinion that the Constitution was a "compact" between the states, each of which had the right to pass on the constitutionality of the federal government's acts. In the case of federal laws that were unfair or unfavorable to particular states, the Kentucky Resolution declared: "It is the right and duty of the several states to nullify those acts, and to protect their citizens from their operations."

By summer's end, Calhoun had developed the doctrine of nullification, which he published in a pamphlet. In it, he proclaimed the right of any state to overrule or modify not only the tariff but also any federal law deemed unconstitutional. Nullification was a complete theory of government that placed the greatest powers on the state level rather than the national. With this proclamation of states' rights, Calhoun had come full circle in his political philosophy.

Calhoun's doctrine failed to produce the results he had anticipated. It alarmed the North and antagonized President Jackson, who saw nullification as a knife poised over the Union's vitals. Jackson made his sympathies clear with a toast at a gathering just after nullification was unveiled on the Senate floor. "Our Federal Union!" said Old Hickory. "It *must* and *shall be* preserved!" Calhoun, forced to hoist his own standard, could only respond: "The Federal Union—next to our liberty, the most dear."

The showdown over the nullification issue came in 1832, when a South Carolina convention formally disallowed two federal tariff acts. President Jackson labeled that action treasonous and immediately called South Carolina's bluff by threatening to use force to ensure obedience to the tariff law. Calhoun and his fellow nullifiers were unable to muster support from the other Southern states, and they finally accepted a compromise tariff

of lower rates. Calhoun had learned a lesson—that it would take a group of states to make the doctrine of states' rights stick. He began at once to recruit followers and to spread the gospel of Southern solidarity.

Even as Calhoun campaigned for Southern unity, opposition to slavery came of age in the 1830s, winning acceptance in a period of reform and religious revivalism. The various antislavery factions still adhered to different principles and goals, which prevented cooperation, not to mention consolidation. Nevertheless, all the groups were backed by a sympathetic press and separately made many converts in their furious efforts to rid the nation of slavery.

The most important antislavery factions were groups of abolitionists; they wanted slavery outlawed and the freed blacks absorbed into society on an equal footing with whites. Besides these social idealists, a group of political pragmatists plumped for abolition only in the new territories, thinking slavery would eventually perish in the Southern states. And there were numerous emancipationists. Like the abolitionists, they demanded that the slaves be freed. But they wanted no part of the freed slaves as fellow citizens; far better, they said, to ship all blacks to Africa. One emancipationist organization, the American Colonization Society, raised large sums of money to ship freed blacks to Liberia. An African nation was set up in 1847 to receive more freed slaves.

Of all the antislavery groups, the abolitionists were the most vigorous and vociferous promoters of their cause. Angry and eloquent, they damned slavery as a sin and slaveowners as criminals. The fiercest of them all was New Englander William Lloyd

Within the image: DESPOTISM — "a glorious prize, how bright it looks., keep steady my Friends, you shall be exalted" — "one step more and it will be within my grasp" — "a little farther CAL." and we are safe." — "Stop you have gone too far, or by the Eternal, ill hang you all;" — "We must bear the Burthen, whether we are exalted or suspended," — "I tell you what Neighbour, I wont stand it; they are laying too much on us" — DISUNION — DECEPTION — CIVIL WAR — TREASON — S.C. ORDINANCE — NULIFICATION — CONSTITUTION — E PLURIBUS UNUM

John Calhoun, ascending a pedestal of Southern affronts to the Union, reaches for a despot's crown in this Northern cartoon from 1833. At right, President Andrew Jackson warns Calhoun and his fellow separatists to reverse their perilous course.

Garrison, founder of the abolitionist newspaper *The Liberator*. Garrison insisted that opposition to slavery was more vital than the preservation of the Union, and because the Constitution protected slavery, he burned a copy in public, calling the document "a covenant with death and an agreement with hell." Garrison made no apology for his extreme views. "I do not wish to think or speak or write, with moderation," he raged. "I will be as harsh as truth, and as uncompromising as justice. And I will be heard."

Some abolitionists were so daring as to

take their crusade into the camp of the enemy. James G. Birney, a wealthy man who had owned slaves himself, boldly attacked the institution in the slave state of Kentucky. So did emancipationist publisher Cassius M. Clay. Protected somewhat by his fearsome reputation as a duelist and by the two cannon that guarded his office, Clay railed against slavery in his Lexington newspaper. Finally, irate Kentuckians put him out of business by dismantling his press in his absence and shipping it to Cincinnati.

A few abolitionists risked their lives to

An 1857 poster advertises a speech given in Eaton, Ohio, by a clergyman wanted in Kentucky for helping runaway slaves. Many fugitive blacks passed through Kentucky on their way into Ohio and thence to Canada.

help slaves flee north to freedom on the so-called Underground Railroad. The fugitives were smuggled in wagons and led through woods to the farmsteads and city houses of sympathizers; they followed many escape routes, most of them ending in Ohio and Indiana. Workers on the Railroad claimed to have rescued or assisted as many as 100,000 escapees in three decades—undoubtedly a considerable exaggeration, since the South reported only 1,000 escapes a year. Yet the Railroad was invaluable as an inspiration for those who opposed slavery as well as for those who plotted to escape it.

Naturally, the abolitionist campaign enraged the Southerners. And it also frightened them, conjuring the nightmarish possibility of an immense uprising among their more than two million slaves. A small version of such an insurrection occurred in the summer of 1831, when a Virginia slave by the name of Nat Turner led about 70 fellows on a bloody rampage that left 55 whites dead. Turner and 16 of his followers were tried and quickly hanged, and soon afterward the slave states acted to prevent abolitionist rhetoric from sparking much worse disasters. Stiff laws were passed restricting freedom of speech and the press; abolitionist tracts were actually burned in the United States Post Office in Charleston.

Faced with increasing pressures both from without and from within, Southerners closed ranks. It ceased to be safe to whisper even a word against the "peculiar institution," and any stranger suspected of antislavery agitation was likely to be hustled out of town in a coat of tar and feathers. Those humane planters who once had thought of slavery as a temporary aberration now claimed defensively that the institution was a positive

LET THE NORTH AWAKE!

T. B. M'CORMICK

Will Discuss the Immorality, Illegality and Unconstitutionality of

AMERICAN SLAVERY,

And the Duty and Power of the General Government to Abolish it,

IN *Town Hall at Eaton*

AT *7 Ock P.M. April 30th 1857*

Mr. M'CORMICK is the Clergyman for whom the Governor of Kentucky made a Requsition upon the Governor of Indiana, charging him with aiding in the escape of Fugitive Slaves. The Warrant was issued and Mr. M'Cormick is thereby exiled from his home. All are respectfully invited to attend.

good, that it benefited the slave with food, clothing and housing, that it uplifted him with Christian tutelage.

In 1838 John Calhoun endorsed the new Southern attitude: "Many in the South once believed that slavery was a moral and political evil. That folly and delusion are gone. We see it now in its true light, and regard it as the most safe and stable basis for free institutions in the world."

A new political crisis threatened with the beginning of the Mexican War in 1846. Americans from every state rushed to join the Army and to fight in behalf of a jingoistic credo with a newly coined name, Manifest Destiny. The credo excused any and all conquest by declaring that it was the God-given right of Americans to inherit the continent from sea to sea. Although Manifest Destiny was popular nationwide, it was made to order for Southern interests. Some Southern firebrands openly discussed annexing Mexico once the government of Santa Anna surrendered. The country could be broken up into dozens of new slave states. The horizons of the more ardent cotton imperialists extended even to the Spanish colony of Cuba, where slavery conveniently existed. The acquisition of just a few new states for slavery would give the South control of the Senate, where the count presently stood at 15 slave states and 15 free states.

John Calhoun did not share the Southerners' enthusiasm for war with Mexico. He foresaw a bitter dispute over the enticing Mexican spoils, which he called "forbidden fruit." And he was right: Even before the brief conflict with Mexico came to an end, a move was made in Congress that sent Northerners and Southerners to their political ram-

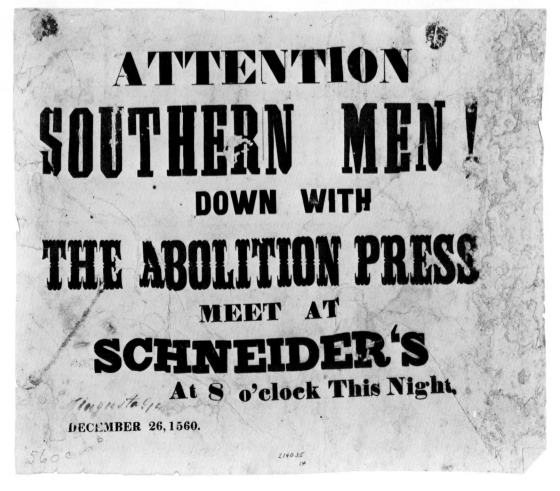

An angry Southern handbill, hastily produced with a misprinted date, announces a rally in Augusta, Georgia, to protest the torrent of antislavery tracts from the North. Southern reaction to the abolitionist movement grew so violent that local people who opposed slavery went underground or moved north.

parts for the third time in as many decades.

The provocation came from David Wilmot, a slovenly, profane, tobacco-chewing country lawyer from Pennsylvania. He introduced a measure proposing that "neither slavery or involuntary servitude shall ever exist" in any territory that might be acquired as a result of the Mexican War. The Wilmot Proviso never made its way into law: Over a span of six months it passed the House twice, but it failed in the Senate. Nevertheless, its impact was staggering. It split Congress along sectional lines, with nearly all members voting on the measure not as Democrats or Whigs—the two major parties of the day—but as Northerners or Southerners. An unsuccessful Southern attempt to quash the proviso in the House demonstrated the extent of the rift: 74 Southerners and four Northerners voted to table Wilmot's measure, 91 Northerners and three Southerners voted to keep it alive. "As if by magic," a Boston journalist wrote of the proviso, "it brought to a head the great question which is about to divide the American people."

Calhoun, his health now failing, was shaken by the Wilmot Proviso and its naked effort to limit the extension of slavery. But he was well enough to enunciate the Southern view when, with the signing of the Treaty of Guadalupe Hidalgo in 1848, Mexico ceded to the United States an immense domain of nearly one million square miles, including all the territory between Texas and the Pacific. Calhoun argued that the territories were not federal property but the joint possession of the individual states, and that Congress therefore had no authority to intervene on the question of slavery. And since slaves were no more than chattel, the Southerners should be as free to transport them to new

territories as others were to move with their mules and oxen. He declared: "I am a Southern man and a slaveholder. I say, for one, I would rather meet any extremity upon earth than give up one inch of our equality—one inch of what belongs to us as members of this great republic!"

The controversy hung like a black cloud over Congress. In both houses, routine was often shattered by invective and threats of disunion. Calhoun warned his sectional rivals, "The North must give way, or there will be a rupture." Congressman Robert Toombs of Georgia, a large-hearted bull of a man, proclaimed his attachment to the Union but then warned, "I do not hesitate to avow before this House and the country, and in the presence of the living God, that if by your legislation you seek to drive us from the territories of California and New Mexico and to abolish slavery in this District, thereby attempting to fix a national degradation upon half the states of this Confederacy, I am for disunion."

Northerners in Congress answered quickly in kind. Senator Salmon P. Chase of Ohio declared, "No menace of disunion will move us from the path which in our judgment it is due to ourselves and the people whom we represent to pursue." Congressman John P. Hale of New Hampshire refused to consider any further compromise. He cried, "If this Union, with all its advantages, has no other cement than the blood of human slavery, let it perish!"

In the meantime, the issue of the extension of slavery caught the eye of recently elected President Zachary Taylor, the hero of the Mexican War. Taylor was a Louisianian and a slaveowner, but he was first and foremost an old general who wanted to serve his coun-

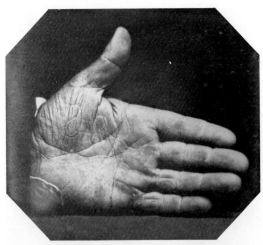

try. And with a soldier's naïve disregard for political protocol, he sought and found a simple solution to the problem.

In 1849, California and New Mexico were still being administered by military officers. Neither had been authorized to organize a territorial government, under whose aegis each region would prepare for statehood. It was during this fledgling stage before statehood that the issue of slavery was most volatile; because a territory was still a ward of the federal government, the U.S. Congress could meddle in any decision made by the territorial government.

As it happened, California, thanks to the gold rush, already had far more than the 60,000 people required for statehood. Since every established state had an unchallenged right to decide for itself the status of slavery, Taylor decided to get California, and later New Mexico, to apply for statehood without going through the territorial phase, thus removing the federal government from the troublesome slavery decision.

Taylor sent agents to California and New Mexico to persuade the settlers there to make application for statehood. California, very much in need of civil government to estab-

lish order in the unruly gold camps, complied gladly with the President's proposal. By November of 1849 a constitution had been drawn up and California had opted to enter the Union as a free state. New Mexico made a start on a similar procedure.

When the proslavery Southerners woke up to Taylor's maneuverings, they could scarcely believe what was taking place. They saw a betrayal by one of their own, a President whom they had expected to protect their sectional interests. They accused Taylor of pressuring California into applying for statehood before the citizens really wanted it. They voiced a suspicion that the President was conspiring with Northern zealots to deny the South any rights in the new territories. They threatened secession. Northerners tried to pacify them with the argument that the Mexican lands were unfavorable for slavery anyway. But Alexander H. Stephens of Georgia retorted that a principle was involved. "Principles, sir, are not only outposts, but the bulwarks of all Constitutional liberty; and if these be yielded, or taken by superior force, the citadel will soon follow."

All the angry Southern voices only provoked familiar rhetoric from the Northerners. "The North is determined that slavery shall not pollute the soil of lands now free, even if it should come to a dissolution of the Union," an Ohio newspaper proclaimed. Slavery, said Senator William Upham of Vermont, was "a crime against humanity, and a sore evil in the body politic."

It seemed that the country would surely break apart. From Mississippi came a summons to Southern states to meet in Nashville in June 1850 to draw up a plan for dealing with the "gross injustice" of the North. But then men of moderation on both sides turned

Margaret Garner, a runaway slave cornered in a room in Cincinnati, shows her captors the bodies of two of her children. It was said that she killed the pair rather than see them returned to bondage; presumably she was interrupted before she could slay her two other children.

for a solution to Henry Clay, the so-called Great Pacificator. Clay was aged and ailing, but his stature and oratory still could sway intransigent partisans.

In January of 1850, Clay presented his solution to the gravest crisis of the half century. He proposed that California should be allowed to enter the Union as a free state, just as it wished, but that Congress should refrain from intervening in the slavery question in any other new territories carved from the Mexican cession. Clay also offered resolutions on three side issues that had cropped up during the debate: that Texas be compensated for yielding certain western tracts to New Mexico, that the sale of slaves be abolished in the District of Columbia, and that Congress enact stiff new laws to assist slaveowners in

the capture and return of runaway slaves.

Clay defended his compromise plan in a series of speeches in the Senate; for each address, the gallery was packed with citizens who sensed that the occasion would be Clay's swan song. The old Kentuckian was nothing less than magnificent. In his rich voice he called for reason. He urged Southerners not to complain if the state of California rejected slavery. And he demanded of Northerners: "What do you want, you who reside in the free states? Have you not your desire in California? And in all human probability you will have it in New Mexico also. What more do you want? You have got what is worth more than a thousand Wilmot Provisos." Clay pointed out that Northerners had nature on their side and facts on their side—that the territories in question had no slavery and were unsuited to slavery. He ended by warning Southern extremists that secession would mean nothing less than war, and he begged them "to pause at the edge of the precipice, before the fearful and disastrous leap is taken into the yawning abyss below."

Clay's plea for moderation was countered on March 4 by John Calhoun, now dying of tuberculosis. (He had less than a month to live.) He was so weak that a colleague had to read his speech. In it Calhoun never mentioned Clay or the compromise measures; instead, he called on the North, as the stronger section of the country, to make concessions to preserve the Union. The North, he said, should grant slaveowners equal rights in the territories of the new West, quiet the abolitionist agitation against slavery and guarantee the return of fugitive slaves. Barring those concessions, Calhoun proposed that the North and the South separate and each section govern itself in peace. If that were not possible, he warned the North, "We shall know what to do, when you reduce the question to submission or resistance."

Calhoun's challenge was met by the magisterial Daniel Webster, in what was perhaps his finest speech. He began, "I wish to speak today, not as a Massachusetts man, nor as a Northern man, but as an American, and a member of the Senate of the United States. I speak today for the preservation of the Union. Hear me for my cause." Webster implored the Northern radicals to soften their position. The Wilmot Proviso, that "taunt or reproach" to the South, was unnecessary because conditions in the West were unfavorable to slavery. "I would not take pains to reaffirm an ordinance of nature," he stated, "nor to reenact the will of God."

Webster's speech was considered a betrayal by the abolitionists, but its message of moderation received high praise elsewhere. Even the fiery Charleston *Mercury* lauded his effort: "With such a spirit as Mr. Webster has shown, it no longer seems impossible to bring this sectional contest to a close." Under the able direction of Senator Stephen A. Douglas of Illinois, Clay's proposals ran the legislative gantlet and were enacted into law by September.

Clay's Compromise of 1850 was hailed as the Union's salvation. A schism had been averted, and Americans, now breathing a bit more easily, looked ahead hopefully to a future free of sectional rancor. Indeed, the compromise strengthened the Southern moderates and thereby helped thwart the plans of belligerent Southern agitators to forge a bloc of separatist Southern states.

But far from curing the nation's ills, the compromise contained a minor measure that would do major damage to the chances for a lasting settlement. That measure was the Fugitive Slave Law.

Runaway slaves were not a serious problem for planters; not many more than a thousand escaped each year, even with the help of the Underground Railroad, and relatively few of them were able to reach sanctuary in the North. Even so, the Fugitive Slave Law was designed to mollify the South, and it did so with some of the harshest national regulations yet instituted by Congress. It placed the full power of the federal government behind efforts to recapture escaped slaves. It created federal police power: A cadre of U.S. commissioners was authorized to issue warrants for the arrest and return of runaways. And it empowered the commissioners to dragoon citizens into slave-catching posses.

The intervention of the federal government in the plight of escaped slaves infuriated even moderate Northerners. Ralph Waldo Emerson called the fugitive measure a "filthy law," and many Northerners vowed to resist it. Not even the U.S. Army could enforce the law, predicted Ohio Congressman Joshua Giddings: "Let the President drench our land of freedom in blood; but he will never make us obey that law."

Once the Fugitive Slave Law was on the books, it was no longer enough for a runaway to reach the North. Professional slave hunters, armed with affidavits from Southern courts, scoured Northern cities, not only ferreting out runaways but sometimes kidnapping free blacks, of whom almost 200,000 lived in Northern communities. Runaways who had felt secure in New York and Philadelphia and Boston were frightened enough to take flight across the Canadian border.

Others fought back. Blacks and whites in Northern cities formed vigilance committees to protect fugitives from the slave catchers. Boston was virtually in a state of insurrection, with abolitionist mobs roaming the streets and influential abolitionist clergymen advocating civil disobedience to the slave-catching municipal police. A Boston slave couple named William and Ellen Craft were whisked from the reach of a Georgia lawman who had come to get them. Fred Wilkins, a black waiter who was being held in a federal courthouse in Boston, was spirited away by a crowd of blacks who burst through the doors of the courthouse.

Then came the wrenching case of Anthony Burns, a Virginia escapee who had been working in a Boston clothing store. When Burns was arrested by a federal marshal,

Escaped slave Josiah Henson, famous as the model for Harriet Beecher Stowe's character Uncle Tom, lectured to abolitionist audiences on his life in bondage.

The Webb family (*below*) toured the Northern states giving dramatic readings of *Uncle Tom's Cabin*. Mary Webb (*center*) took her act to England, where the novel had sold one million copies within a year of its publication in 1852.

abolitionists held a mass meeting at Faneuil Hall and were whipped into action by fiery oratory. "I want that man set free in the streets of Boston," shouted Wendell Phillips, the well-born reform lecturer. "If that man leaves the city of Boston, Massachusetts is a conquered state."

The crowd stormed the federal courthouse where Burns was being held. In the melee a special deputy was killed, and the federal marshals and deputies were hard put to restrain the mob. Finally, the federal government sent in Regular Army troops to take Burns out. With flags flying at half-mast and bells tolling a dirge, Burns was marched through crepe-hung streets to the harbor and put aboard a Virginia-bound ship.

"When it was all over," a Boston attorney wrote, "and I was left alone in my office, I put my face in my hands and wept. I could do nothing less." Countless Northerners were galvanized by Burns's fate. "We went to bed one night old-fashioned, conservative, Compromise Union Whigs," wrote one, "and waked up stark mad abolitionists." Popular outrage stirred the North to legal action. Nine states passed personal-liberty laws designed to frustrate the Fugitive Slave Law and protect blacks in their domain. Southern slave hunters found it so difficult to prove their case and to get cooperation from Northern authorities that most gave up the chase.

The plight of the runaways inspired and brought to publication in 1852 the ultimate piece of abolitionist propaganda. This work, a novel by a meek and pious New Englander named Harriet Beecher Stowe, was *Uncle Tom's Cabin, or Life among the Lowly*.

As literature, the book suffered from a contrived plot and stereotyped characters. Yet it personalized the evils of slavery, and the suffering of Uncle Tom and Eliza and Little Eva tugged at the heartstrings of readers who had been unmoved by abolitionist rhetoric. The book became a bestseller almost overnight; within a year 300,000 copies were sold, and the story reached an even wider audience in the form of a drama, which dozens of touring troupes performed in lyceums and in meeting halls all over the country. Meanwhile, Southern readers ground their teeth over Mrs. Stowe's claims that their society was evil; their rage and frustration strengthened the garrison mentality that had gripped the South.

So it was that the United States at mid-century stood in grave peril. Opposition to slavery had permeated and pervaded the North; few Northerners knew of or cared about the Southern planters' plight. In the South, the commitment to slavery was now inalterable. It did not matter that only about 350,000 people—one family out of four—actually owned slaves. Most Southern whites firmly believed that their livelihood, their dear institutions and traditions, and indeed their personal safety amid almost four million blacks all depended on preserving and extending the use of slave labor.

The meager chances for a rapprochement between the North and the South were further dimmed in 1852. Henry Clay and Daniel Webster followed John Calhoun to the grave, leaving their constituencies in the hands of less seasoned, less wise, less patient leaders. At the same time a new ingredient was added to the North-South quarrels—an ingredient that gave Americans everywhere a preview of their future. It was organized violence, and it erupted in Kansas.

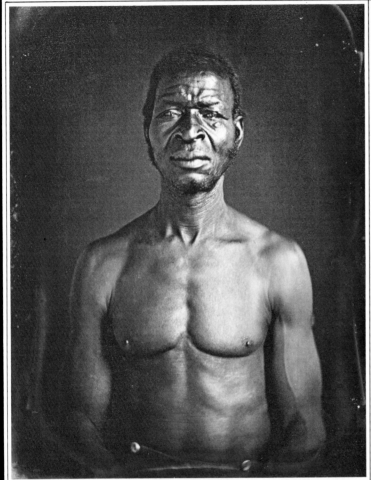

JACK, A SLAVE DRIVER

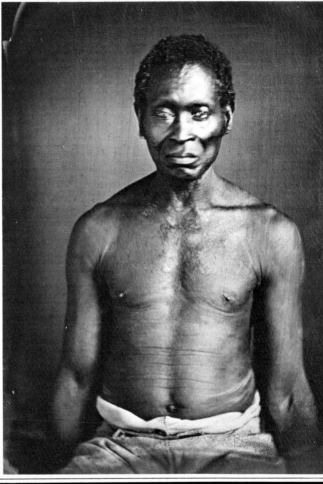

FASSENA, A CARPENTER

To Be a Slave

"I'd ruther be dead than be a nigger on one of these big plantations," a white Mississippian told a Northern visitor. For those who were slaves, the plantation life often did lead prematurely to the grave.

Born into bondage, very likely sold at least once during the course of his or her lifetime, a slave normally began to work in the fields by the age of 12. From that point on, overwork was his daily portion. One former slave said of his servitude on a Louisiana plantation: "The hands are required to be in the cotton field as soon as it is light in the morning, and, with the exception of 10 or 15 minutes, which is given them at noon, they are not permitted to be a moment idle until it is too dark to see, and when the moon is full, they often labor till the middle of the night."

The majority of slaves were fed poorly; many subsisted chiefly on a "hog and hominy" diet, which consisted of a peck of corn and about three pounds of fatty salted meat a week. They were generally clothed in shabby homespun or in cheap fabrics known as "Negro cloth," which were man-

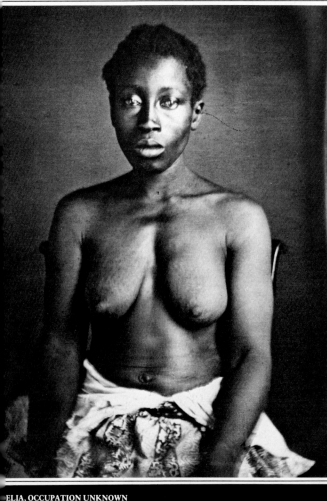

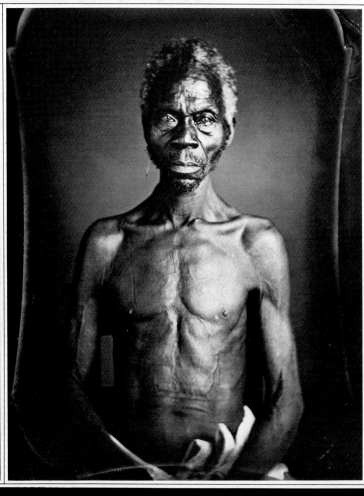

ELIA, OCCUPATION UNKNOWN

RENTY, A FIELD SLAVE

factured in Northern or English spinning mills. Children wore only shirts and went hoeless even in winter.

From six to 12 slaves were quartered in each leaky, drafty, dirt-floored one-room hack. "Their houses," wrote an Alabama physician, "can be but laboratories of disease." What medical care slaves received was primitive at best. Malaria, yellow fever, cholera, tuberculosis, typhoid, typhus, tetanus and pneumonia took terrible tolls. Many slaves were afflicted with worms,

four out of 100 lived to be 60 years of age. Slaves were kept in a state of fear by punishment and the threat of punishment. They were required to show abject humility when they addressed whites: They had to bow their heads and lower their gaze. No wonder that slaves—even those who received relatively good treatment—yearned for freedom. "O, that I were free!" wrote a slave who finally managed to escape. "O, God, save me! I will run away. Get caught or get clear. I had as well be killed running

Four slaves gaze impassively from daguerreotypes taken in South Carolina in 1850. The pictures among the earliest known photographs of slaves were part of a study on racial characteristics conducted by scientist Louis Agassiz

Stripped, Prodded and Paraded

Slaves approached the auction block in dreadful uncertainty, fearing the worst. Nothing in their dreary lives was quite so frightening, or so degrading.

The slaves, freshly scrubbed and dressed in clean clothes, were paraded in front of the white shoppers, who sometimes made them jump or dance to show their liveliness. Young men and women were often stripped, partly to show that they had never been whipped. "The customers would feel our bodies," recalled a former slave, "and make us show our teeth, precisely as a jockey examines a horse."

Trade cards like this one, advertising the services of professional slave auctioneers, were widely displayed in Southern towns.

Davenport Ellis. **Lewis Livingston.**

ELLIS & LIVINGSTON,

AUCTION AND COMMISSION DEPOT,

FOR THE SALE OF

NEGROES.

COLUMBUS,-----GEORGIA,

☞ We neither buy nor sell NEGROES on our own account ☜

A numbered identification tag, attached to the slave by the auctioneer, was keyed to a full description that was presented with the bill.

At a slave sale in Richmond, the auctioneer (*left*) accepts a bid for a female slave while prospective buyers examine other blacks awaiting sale. A few traders had special rooms for displaying "choice stock"— pretty quadroons and octoroons who fetched up to $2,500 or more from New Orleans brothel owners.

The Breakup of a Slave Family

Slave families are broken up at a railroad station in Richmond. In most cases, slaves were sold between October and May so that they could become accustomed to their new plantations in time for the next growing season.

A slave family sent to auction was seldom sold to a single buyer. And so followed the breakup every slave expected: a child taken from its mother, a couple separated.

The slave family was a tenuous unit to begin with; from the master's viewpoint, couples existed to produce more slaves to be put to work or sold for profit. A man and woman might be matched for breeding purposes against their will. With the master's permission, the couple might have a wedding ceremony, though slave marriage had no status in law. Since the union might soon be broken up by one partner's sale, a preacher changed the marital vow to say, "Until death or distance do you part."

A dealer's broadside announces his willingness to purchase slaves for cash. Many a slave was sold without warning to pay the debts of his owner.

CASH!

All persons that have SLAVES to dispose of, will do well by giving me a call, as I will give the

HIGHEST PRICE FOR

Men, Women, & CHILDREN.

Any person that wishes to sell, will call at Hill's tavern, or at Shannon Hill for me, and any information they want will be promptly attended to.

Thomas Griggs.

Charlestown, May 7, 1835.

PRINTED AT THE FREE PRESS OFFICE, CHARLESTOWN.

A prosperous planter (below, right) sells a young mulatto— his own illegitimate son.

A Slave's Sense of Caste

"Go along, half-priced nigger!" one sla[ve] joshed another. "You wouldn't fetch $5[00] and I'm worth $1,000." The gibe was goo[d] natured but had a sharp edge. "Ever[y] body," explained a former slave, "war[ted] the privilege of whipping somebody else[.]"

The division of plantation labor foster[ed] a slave caste system. The slave aristocra[cy] were the skilled craftsmen, the house se[r]vants who served the master and his famil[y] and the so-called drivers—field foreme[n.] At the bottom of the social ladder we[re] the unskilled field hands. And even t[he] lowly field hands felt superior to slaves wh[o] worked in coal mines.

Some slaves used another criterion of st[a]tus, ancestry, to claim a modicum of respe[ct] or a better job. One Georgia slave of mix[ed] blood asked her owner to relieve her of fie[ld] labor "on account of her color."

A house slave prepares a meal amid the clutter of a plantation kitchen. Kitchen workers, who had access to extra food, were popular and important among the slaves.

In an 1840s daguerreotype (*left*) from Louisiana, a nurse holds her master's child. The planters' children often depended on their "mammy" for affection and deferred to her even as adults.

A groom feeds his mistress's horse in a painted collage known as a "pastie." This pastie and the one below were made in the 1840s for the children of a Mississippi family; their mother was the horsewoman shown above.

A collage entitled *Hauling the Whole Week's Picking* depicts field slaves of various ages. Most masters used a fraction system to rate the slaves' work capacity. Children began as "quarter hands" and worked their way up to "half hands" and "full hands." Elderly slaves started sliding back down the scale.

Precious Hours of Free Time

Slaves were usually granted time off on Sundays, and sometimes on Saturday afternoons. Most of them spent these precious hours cleaning their own houses, tending their gardens, or working on other plantations for a little money. The remainder of their time was devoted to simple pleasures.

They went fishing, fashioned baskets or brooms, danced to the music of a banjo or fiddle. Some slaves were satisfied to go to prayer meetings or simply to savor the luxury of having nothing to do. Said a free black of a slave he had known: "Her idea of the joy of heaven was simply rest."

Slave children pass time by their cabins. They grew up on black folktales such as the Br'er Rabbit stories, in which the weak use cunning to overcome the strong.

Slaves enjoy a holiday dance in this idealized painting. Although many planters sponsored festivities at Christmas time, few of their slaves were as well dressed as these.

Slaves gather around a coffin to mourn the death of a fellow. Burials were frequently held at night because of work requirements; weeks later on a rest day, joyous funeral celebrations were held to sing, drink and dance the dead to heaven

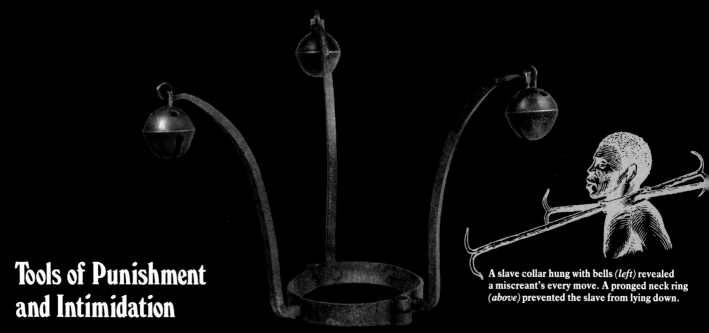

A slave collar hung with bells (*left*) revealed a miscreant's every move. A pronged neck ring (*above*) prevented the slave from lying down.

Tools of Punishment and Intimidation

"He has been gelded, and is not yet well," wrote a Louisiana jailer after capturing a runaway slave. Although this barbaric punishment was used to control only the most unruly blacks, nearly all slaves endured some form of brutal coercion at some time.

Almost all the large plantations were equipped with various instruments of punishment, and masters who were squeamish hired "slave breakers" to apply them forcefully. The most common implement was a long rawhide whip. Blows from this whip took the skin off the back of a stripped and spread-eagled offender. Standard punishment was 15 to 20 lashes, but the number for serious offenses often ran into the hundreds. To prevent infection, whip wounds were sluiced with salt water, and the resulting pain was excruciating. At the mere recollection of it, a former slave wrote, "The flesh crawls upon my bones."

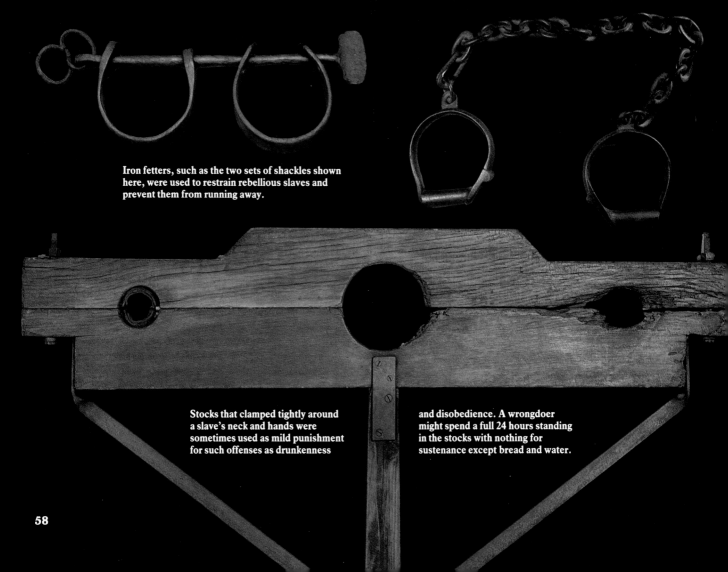

Iron fetters, such as the two sets of shackles shown here, were used to restrain rebellious slaves and prevent them from running away.

Stocks that clamped tightly around a slave's neck and hands were sometimes used as mild punishment for such offenses as drunkenness and disobedience. A wrongdoer might spend a full 24 hours standing in the stocks with nothing for sustenance except bread and water.

A whip of chain and leather has a spiked handle (*left*) for administering clublike blows. A canvas paddle coated with rubber (*below*) did the work of a whip without tearing up a slave's back.

Stripped naked, a slave receives a brutal whipping in front of other slaves. After several blows, the lash usually became wet with blood; as the beating continued, the victim's cries of pain turned into low moans.

A statement signed by a Kentucky official certifies that a professional slave breaker is owed four dollars for whipping eight slaves.

A gruesome network of scars on a slave's back bears witness to a severe whipping—or several. The slave in this photograph escaped during the War and fought as a soldier in the Union Army.

The Urge to Escape: a Troublesome 'Disease of the Mind"

According to a Louisiana doctor, blacks suffered from a peculiar "disease of the mind" that caused them to run away from their masters, and the proper cure was "whipping the devil out of them." Whippings, along with curfews and antifugitive patrols, did keep down the number of runaways. But slaves continued to run away.

Often, the fugitive had been recently sold to another plantation and was trying to return to his family. Others fled grueling labor or a cruel overseer. Some runaways sought freedom in the distant North. Whatever drove them, only small numbers made good their escape, often with the help of the Underground Railroad. Most fugitives were captured after a few days at large.

Some runaways chose death over recapture. A Louisiana fugitive caught on a raft on the Mississippi refused to surrender, and so he was shot. "He fell at the third fire," a white reported. "So determined was he not to be captured that when an effort was made to rescue him from drowning, he made battle with his club and sunk waving his weapon in angry defiance."

Exhausted fugitives reach a farm in Newport, Indiana, a way station on the Underground Railroad to Canada. "I feel lighter," said one slave. "The dread is gone."

Crusaders for Freedom

A shackled slave begging for freedom was the poignant emblem of the abolitionist cause. This lithograph appeared on a broadside with a poem by John Greenleaf Whittier, "Our Countrymen in Chains."

Abolitionism, the militant movement that turned most Northerners against slavery, was born in a jail in 1830. At that time, more than a hundred antislavery groups were already at work—but with more high-mindedness than heat: Their members, like generations of moralists and humanitarians before them, patiently called for improvement in the slaves' lot in preparation for emancipation at some later date. Antislavery efforts began changing fast, however, when William Lloyd Garrison, a 24-year-old editor from Massachusetts, was released from jail in Baltimore in June of 1830, after serving seven weeks for libeling a merchant who was legally ferrying slaves up and down the coast.

During his imprisonment Garrison made an angry resolve to end slavery—not later, but now. Returning to Boston, he started publishing *The Liberator* on New Year's Day, 1831. Though the newspaper would never exceed a circulation of 3,000, it enlisted hundreds of gifted followers in the abolitionist crusade and infused them with Garrison's tireless, fearless, selfless zeal. With several friends, Garrison in 1833 founded the American Anti-Slavery Society, whose membership rose to nearly 250,000 in 1838. This was the first American organization in which women as well as men, and blacks as well as whites, played an active role.

The organization operated on a shoestring; its main asset—often its only one—was the time members gave to making speeches, distributing literature and collecting signatures on petitions to Congress. The leading crusaders, 12 of whom are vignetted on the following pages, were not content merely to demand freedom and equality for blacks. Many espoused other radical causes: women's rights, prison reform, amelioration of the harsh debtors' laws, temperance, pacifism.

Risk and adversity were standard fare for society members. They ran safe houses on the Underground Railroad and defied mobs of workers who feared that emancipation would bring hordes of freed slaves to take their jobs. The members' strident campaigning made them distasteful to polite Northerners, even those who shared their two basic beliefs—that slavery was a sin and that everyone was his brother's keeper. Garrison and a few extremists alienated reverent, patriotic folk by attacking organized religion and advocating civil disobedience.

The Anti-Slavery Society thrived on opposition, but internal dissension was another story: The society was fragmented by clashes among its aggressive leaders and their multiple causes. For example, when Garrison insisted on electing a woman to the executive board, three cofounders went off in a huff to start a rival organization. Others left to promote abolition through the Liberty Party, which ran James G. Birney for President in 1840 (and polled only 7,000 votes). But by then the drive for abolition had built up irreversible momentum.

Garrison enjoyed the first taste of victory years before emancipation became the law of the land. In 1855, after decades of arguing that true equality was impossible as long as the races were kept separate by law, he and several colleagues persuaded the state of Massachusetts to open its public schools and public transportation to all races.

Members of the American Anti-Slavery Society rally outdoors in Syracuse, New York, in this rare early photo from the 1840s. The speaker, at center, is believed to be philanthropist Gerrit Smith; seated in front of him is Frederick Douglass, the fugitive slave turned abolitionist orator.

Leaders in the War against Slavery

Frederick Douglass

"I appear this evening as a thief and a robber," announced Frederick Douglass, a self-taught fugitive slave, at an anti-slavery meeting in 1842. "I stole this head, these limbs, this body from my master, and ran off with them." With just such pathos and outrage Douglass evoked the suffering of slaves in uncounted speeches, in his autobiography and in *The North Star*, a weekly newspaper he founded and edited for 17 years in Rochester, New York. Originally convinced that abolition should be achieved by "moral suasion" alone, without political action, Douglass eventually joined the Liberty Party. He never stopped campaigning for complete black equality. At the end of his long life, when asked for a word of advice for a young man just starting out, he replied: "Agitate!"

Theodore Parker

Theodore Parker, a scholarly Congregational minister, attacked the Fugitive Slave Law from his Boston pulpit, urging his parishioners to aid runaways in any way they could. And Parker did more than preach. Serving as a leader of the Boston Vigilance Committee, he concealed scores of fugitives from the federal agents deputized to recapture them, and he engineered their escapes to Canada. Parker justified his criminal conduct on purely religious grounds. "The Fugitive Slave Law contradicts the acknowledged precepts of the Christian religion," he declared in 1851. "It violates the noblest instincts of humanity; it asks us to trample on the law of God. It commands what nature, religion, and God alike forbid; it forbids what nature, religion, and God alike command."

Sojourner Truth

An illiterate slave who ran away from her New York master in the 1820s, Isabella Baumfree began calling herself Sojourner Truth in the 1840s because, as she later told Harriet Beecher Stowe, God intended her to "travel up an' down de land, showin' de people der sins, an' bein' a sign unto dem." Tall, gaunt and dynamic, she became a popular speaker at abolitionist rallies. Her plain speaking about the evils of slavery moved many audiences, and her wit silenced those who dared challenge her. After one speech, a listener demanded, "Old woman, do you think that your talk about slavery does any good? Why, I don't care any more for your talk than I do for the bite of a flea."

"Perhaps not," replied Sojourner Truth, "but, de Lord willin', I'll keep you scratchin'."

William Lloyd Garrison

The radical genius of the movement, William Lloyd Garrison was arrogant and relentless in preaching against slavery and inequality. Conviction alone, not status or wealth, made him so self-assured; he had been abandoned by his drunken immigrant father and had eked out a living as an apprentice cobbler, carpenter and printer. He went on to become a newspaper editor and dabble in politics, backing the commercial interests he later attacked with such virulence. After his conversion to abolitionism, he borrowed some type and, in the autumn of 1830, published the manifesto to which he devoted the rest of his life:

"The liberty of a people is the gift of God and nature."

"That which is not just is not law."

"He who oppugns public liberty overthrows his own."

Harriet Beecher Stowe

The author of *Uncle Tom's Cabin* was the pious daughter, wife, sister and mother of ministers, and she could not help preaching herself, even though she was self-effacing to a fault. She advocated abolition in the belief that slavery jeopardized Christian souls. "Such peril and shame as now hangs over this country is worse than Roman slavery," she wrote in 1851, adding mildly, "I hope every woman who can write will not be silent." Her modesty was unshaken by the enormous success of her novel. If anything made her vulnerable to the sin of pride, it was praise from arch-abolitionist William Lloyd Garrison. "I estimate the value of anti-slavery writing by the abuse it brings," he wrote her after reading her book. "Now all the defenders of slavery have let me alone and are abusing you."

Charles Calistus Burleigh

At 24, lawyer Charles Burleigh became an agent and influential lecturer for Massachusetts' Middlesex Anti-Slavery Society. In answer to those who feared that newly freed slaves would inundate the North and undercut the wages of white workers, Burleigh argued that blacks would stop coming north once they were freed, and that wage-earning blacks would increase the market for Northern products. Further, he argued that with education a free black would work far harder than any slave and prove more valuable to society: "As much as brain and muscle are worth more than muscle only; as much as moral joined to mental power is a better wealth than mere brute force; so much will the emancipation of a nation's slaves enrich the nation. Why, then, should not our slaves go free?"

Lucretia Mott

Quaker minister Lucretia Mott helped found the Philadelphia Female Anti-Slavery Society in 1833. With her abolitionist husband, she supported the work of the Underground Railroad, harboring runaways in her Philadelphia home. In her lectures she called for boycotting the agricultural products of slavery, and she dared to take her antislavery message into Virginia. In 1840, she attended London's World Anti-Slavery Convention, and when women were denied an active part in the proceedings, she became an ardent feminist. In keeping with her Quaker heritage, Mrs. Mott was a confirmed pacifist; she would use any tactic but outright violence to oppose injustice to slaves. She declared, "I am no advocate of passivity. Quakerism does not mean quietism."

Charles Lenox Remond

Born free in Salem, Massachusetts, Charles Remond was the first black to address public meetings on behalf of abolition. As an agent of the Massachusetts chapter of the American Anti-Slavery Society, he canvassed New England and in 1840 represented the parent organization at the first World Anti-Slavery Convention in London. Back home after a 19-month lecture tour of Great Britain and Ireland, Remond became famous for his powerful speeches. Not content with emancipation, Remond demanded that blacks be rewarded in proportion to their contributions to society. To do anything less, he told Massachusetts legislators in 1842, was an "unkind and unchristian policy calculated to make every man disregardful of his conduct, and every woman unmindful of her reputation."

Wendell Phillips

The scion of one of Boston's wealthiest and most influential families, Wendell Phillips was converted to the cause of abolitionism by his future wife in 1836. He abandoned the practice of law, which he considered boring, and quickly became one of the outstanding orators of the antislavery movement. Following in the radical footsteps of William Lloyd Garrison, Phillips cursed the Constitution for permitting the existence of slavery and refused to support it by running for public office—or even voting. He stopped short of advocating violence but did call for the Northern states to secede from the Union rather than put up with Southern slavery any longer, declaring, "If lawful and peaceful efforts for the abolition of slavery in our land will dissolve it, let the Union go."

Harriet Tubman

A Maryland slave who ran away in 1849, tiny, fearless Harriet Tubman earned the *nom de guerre* "Moses" for leading more than 300 slaves to freedom on the Underground Railroad. She was so skillful at disguise and evasion that she was never caught, nor were any of the fugitives in her charge. In the War she served the Union Army as cook, laundress, nurse and spy. Because she worked in secrecy, praise for her successes came first from those who shared her labors. "I have had the applause of the crowd," Frederick Douglass wrote her, "while the most that you have done has been witnessed by a few trembling, scarred and foot-sore bondmen and women, whom you have led out of the house of bondage, and whose heartfelt 'God bless you' has been your only reward."

Maria Weston Chapman

Maria Chapman, a well-to-do matron of Pilgrim stock, was one of the 12 founders of the Boston Female Anti-Slavery Society. She became a disciple of William Lloyd Garrison and edited *The Liberator* when he was away from Boston on lecture tours. Mrs. Chapman showed her courage in 1835, when a mob surrounded the society's meeting place. Since the black members were in particular danger, she told the whites each to take the arm of a black companion; then, two by two, the women marched from the hall. "When we emerged into the open daylight," she recalled, "there went up a roar of rage and contempt, which increased when they saw that we did not intend to separate." Mrs. Chapman calmly led her friends through the mob to her home, where she reconvened the meeting.

John Greenleaf Whittier

The son of a Massachusetts Quaker farmer, John Green-leaf Whittier was an inveterate campaigner for liberal causes. Hundreds of antislavery poems, written between 1833 and 1865, made him the poet laureate of abolition. In his stirring "Stanzas for the Times," Whittier used rhetorical questions to imply that slavery sullied the freedom American patriots had died for: "Is this the land our fathers loved? / The freedom which they toil'd to win?" He warned his readers that they must continue their ancestors' war against tyranny by working to free the slaves or they would eventually sacrifice their own freedom to Southern slaveholders. Shall we, demanded the poet, fairly insisting on "no" as the answer, "Yoke in with marked and branded slaves, / And tremble at the driver's whip?"

The Avenging Angel

"Better that a whole generation of men, women and children should pass away by a violent death than that a word of either [the Bible or the Declaration of Independence] should be violated in this country."

JOHN BROWN

Shortly before midnight on May 24, 1856, James Doyle heard a knock at the door of his cabin near Dutch Henry's Crossing on Pottawatomie Creek in eastern Kansas. Minutes earlier, the settler might have heard his two bulldogs barking, but they were silent now, cut to pieces by the visitors' swords or put to flight. Doyle apparently feared nothing as he opened the door.

Five armed men forced their way into Doyle's house. They demanded that he surrender to their "Army of the North." They took Doyle outside and very likely questioned him about his politics; he was well known locally as a proslavery man. Then a visitor reentered the house and ordered Doyle's two oldest sons, William and Drury, to come outside. Doyle's wife, Mahala, begged that no harm come to her youngest son, 14-year-old John, and he was allowed to remain behind.

Out on the prairie, the visitors cut down and killed James Doyle with their swords. They split his sons' skulls like melons. They sliced the arms off one of the corpses. They kept on hacking at the bloody bodies for a while, and then they departed, to a litany of wails from Mrs. Doyle. John Brown of Osawatomie had come to call.

"Old Man" Brown, as he was called, did not start the violence that was tearing Kansas apart. Others before him had killed to win the new territory for slavery, or to keep slavery out. A few were even avowed terrorists like Brown, men for whom killing was not just a means to an end but an end in itself. But only Brown, starting on that dark night on the Kansas prairie, murdered in the name of the Lord and managed to convince others that killing over the issue of slavery was acceptable and in some wise justified. Indeed, Brown, more clearly than anyone else, argued that slavery was a just cause for war.

Brown's fanatic zeal grew naturally from his troubled origins. His family background was notably unstable. Certain relatives on his mother's side were said to have died mad. His father was a frontiersman, always pulling up stakes and moving on. As a child, John had had little schooling, little love. As a man, he was a chronic failure. He failed at farming, tanning, land speculation and stock breeding. In all, he suffered 15 business failures in four states and weathered numerous lawsuits and accusations of dishonesty.

It was from his stern Calvinist father that Brown inherited his devout hatred of slavery. He yearned to harm slaveowners greatly, to smite them hip and thigh for God. He styled himself the Angel of the Lord, and he meant to be an avenging angel; he openly advocated the use of violence against God's slaveholding enemies and against the bounty hunters enforcing the Fugitive Slave Law. His fire-and-brimstone exhortations won admirers all through the East. "Whenever he spoke," wrote Frederick Douglass, an escaped slave turned abolitionist preacher, "his words commanded earnest attention. His arguments seemed to convince all; his appeals touched all, and his will impressed all."

To those who fell under his spell, John Brown was quite simply intimidating. At 56, he was lean, sinewy and ramrod straight. His associates invariably described him as being six feet tall, though he actually was just five feet nine inches. An awed disciple compared his thin, grim, leathery face to an eagle's—to which one of Brown's sons reportedly added, "or another carnivorous bird." A second son said he looked like a meat ax. And when Brown declared that God had ordered him to "break the jaws of the wicked," his fol-

John Brown, a driven abolitionist, owned this revolver in May 1856, when he and his companions killed five proslavery Kansans in cold blood along Pottawatomie Creek.

lowers believed him and were ready to obey.

Brown's first venture into ritual murder did not end with the butchery at the home of James Doyle. The Old Man and his companions—including four of his seven sons—rode on for half a mile or so to the sod house of Allen Wilkinson, a member of the proslavery territorial legislature. Again there was discussion of where the householder stood on the slavery question, and Brown ordered the man outside. Again a wife pleaded and then waited helplessly while her husband was murdered, a blade run through his side and his skull laid open.

Brown had just one more stop to make now, the James Harris house. He was looking not for Harris himself but for Harris' boss, "Dutch" Henry Sherman, a thuggish saloonkeeper and a known proslavery man. By chance, Dutch Henry was out on the prairie searching for some missing cattle, but his

brother, "Dutch" Bill, was staying overnight at the Harris home. Brown's men split Dutch Bill's skull, ran him through the side and then, in the inexplicable final act of their night of terror, severed one of his hands.

These five killings became known as the Pottawatomie Massacre. Of course, the success did not sate John Brown's sense of murderous mission. He must go on, for—as he was fond of saying—"without the shedding of blood there is no remission of sins." There were sins aplenty to be remitted in Kansas and everywhere in the slave-owning South.

The chain of events that had brought John Brown to Kansas had begun two and a half years earlier. On January 4, 1854, Senator Stephen A. Douglas of Illinois reported out of his Committee on Territories a bill to organize the so-called Nebraska Territory, which included Kansas, in preparation for statehood. Douglas saw Kansas as a thoroughfare for a railroad line to the West Coast, with its eastern terminus in his native state. But as always, slavery was a stumbling block.

The new territory was north of the Missouri Compromise line, which meant that slavery was automatically prohibited. Precisely because of this, Southern Senators had opposed previous attempts to organize the territory and could be expected to do so again. One of them, Senator David R. Atchison of Missouri, vowed that he would rather "sink in hell" than see Kansas enter the Union as a free state.

There seemed to be no way around the problem—no way, that is, until Douglas' bill incorporated the idea of popular sovereignty. In the terms of the bill, the Nebraska and Kansas lands would be admitted to the Union "as their constitution may prescribe at the time of their admission." In other words, it would be left up to the settlers of the territories to choose by their own vote whether or not they wanted slavery.

Douglas was an ambitious man, given rather too much to drink and boast, but he was a great statesman. A firm believer in Manifest Destiny, he knew that the admission of more states to the Union would remain deadlocked so long as the slavery issue divided the North and the South. Indeed, the whole settlement of the Great Plains and the West could be stalled by the sectional controversy—and so could his own drive for the presidency. But if he could unite the country behind the idea of popular sovereignty, then he would stand an excellent chance of winning the White House.

Southern Democrats and other assorted proslavery men were indignant to note a serious flaw in the Douglas bill. It made no mention of the Missouri Compromise, whose terms had not been abrogated. Thus the legislation created an obvious contradiction: The ban on slaves effectively kept out of the territory the slaveowners who would vote for a proslavery constitution at the time Kansas was up for admission to statehood.

The solution was simple enough: In exchange for crucial Southern support for his bill, Douglas accepted an amendment repealing the part of the Missouri Compromise that prohibited slavery north of the 36° 30′ line. "By God, sir, you are right," he reportedly remarked to a Southern Senator. "I will incorporate it into my bill, though I know it will raise a hell of a storm."

The Congressional debate was perhaps the fiercest in American history. In a letter to a Washington newspaper, Senator Salmon P. Chase of Ohio and five of his antislav-ery colleagues denounced Douglas' Kansas-Nebraska bill as "a gross violation of a sacred pledge"; as "a criminal betrayal of precious rights; as part and parcel of an atrocious plot to exclude from the vast unoccupied region immigrants from the Old World and free laborers from our own States, and convert it into a dreary region of despotism, inhabited by masters and slaves." Tempers flared in debate and insults were traded that nearly led to a duel between Congressmen John C. Breckinridge of Kentucky and Francis Cutting of New York. Newspapers fanned the flames. In one satirical poem Douglas was lampooned as a puppet of the South:

The Dropsied Dwarf of Illinois
By brother sneaks called, 'Little Giant'
He who has made so great a noise
By being to the slave power pliant.

The Kansas-Nebraska bill passed the Senate in March and the House two months later. The vote was resolutely sectional. Most Southern members of Congress, whatever their party affiliation, voted "Yea," while nearly all Northerners said "Nay." With passage of the Act, the last vestiges of the truce of 1850 were struck down. Serious trouble was now a certainty, and radicals on both sides rejoiced at the prospect of a showdown. Senator Charles S. Sumner of Massachusetts called the new law "the best bill on which Congress ever acted" because it "makes all future compromises impossible."

The showdown was swift in coming, for whichever side rushed more of its own to the new land would win the upper hand, gaining control of the territorial legislature and with it the authority to write the final word on slavery. Senator William H. Seward of New

Youthful and beardless, John Brown pledges allegiance to an unidentified flag—possibly an abolitionist banner. The photograph, the earliest known picture of Brown, was most likely taken in 1846 in Springfield, Massachusetts. At the time, Brown made a living grading wool for New England textile manufacturers. On the side, he aided runaway slaves, attended abolitionist meetings, and formulated grandiose plans for freeing the South's slave population.

Proslavery Missourians trek to Kansas to cast illegal votes and harass Free Staters. These outlanders were known pejoratively as "Border Ruffians" in the North, but the term became so popular in Missouri that businessmen added it to their company names.

York had made clear the issue and the goal. "Come on then, Gentlemen of the Slave States," he said. "Since there is no escaping your challenge, I accept it in behalf of the cause of freedom. We will engage in competition for the virgin soil of Kansas, and God give the victory to the side which is stronger in numbers as it is in right." Even before the Act passed Congress, Massachusetts had chartered an Emigrant Aid Company to encourage antislavery people to go to Kansas.

The other side was at least as determined to capture Kansas. "When you reside within one day's journey of the territory," roared Senator Atchison to an audience of fellow Missourians, "and when your peace, your quiet and your property depend on your action, you can, without an exertion, send five hundred of your young men who will vote in favor of your institutions." Nor did Atchison expect to stop at mere voting. He confided in a letter to Senator Jefferson Davis of Mississippi, "We will be compelled to shoot, burn and hang, but the thing will soon be over."

In the months following passage of the Act, more and more men made their way to the plains. One of them was Andrew Reeder of Pennsylvania, sent by President Franklin Pierce to be governor of the territory. When Reeder called for the election of a territorial legislature, the situation began to unravel.

A census taken before the voting showed only 2,905 eligible voters. But when the polls closed in March 1855, the tally revealed 6,307 ballots cast, most of them for proslavery candidates. Clearly, Senator Atchison had succeeded in his campaign to flood Kansas with proslavery Missourians; hundreds of the interlopers, called Border Ruffians by the abolitionist press, had come over the line en masse to stuff the ballot boxes. Actually, the trip was unnecessary, for bona fide proslavery settlers far outnumbered their opponents, and the Free State men had further limited their own influence by flocking together around the town of Lawrence.

Reeder was thoroughly intimidated by the Border Ruffians, and so, despite fevered protests from Free Staters, he let the election stand. So did his chief in Washington, President Pierce. Then salt was rubbed in the Free Staters' wounds: The new Kansas legis-

lature, meeting at Shawnee Mission during the summer and autumn, enacted a series of draconian laws designed to protect slavery. Harboring a fugitive slave became a hanging offense; merely expressing doubts about slavery could lead to jail. Capping it all, the proslavery legislators expelled the few Free State members who had been elected.

The Free Staters left in a rage to form their own government. They proceeded to elect a governor, draft a constitution outlawing slavery and apply to Washington for admission to the Union as a free state. This sorry episode cost Governor Reeder his job

Six Kansas Free Staters stand ready to fire their outdated cannon at proslavery troublemakers. Some of the artillery pieces employed in the Kansas conflict were trophies from the Mexican War. Others were even older relics used to fire salutes during Fourth of July celebrations.

for failing to keep order and all but ensured a violent collision between the rival factions.

The collision came in November 1855, when a Free Stater was killed in a land-claim dispute with a slavery advocate. The known killer was not arrested, and the slain man's friends vented their wrath by burning the murderer's home. Action followed reaction until the proslavery sheriff of Douglas County—a man named Samuel Jones—enlisted the aid of a small army of Border Ruffians to help him arrest the Free State men. By early December several hundred raiders had mustered along the Wakarusa River near the Free Staters' town of Lawrence.

The enemies of the Border Ruffians hastily sent out the call to arms. "We want every true Free State man in Kansas at Lawrence immediately," said James Lane, a prominent antislavery partisan who was to be elected a United States Senator. One of those who turned out was John Brown, who had just joined five of his sons in Kansas. Seeing the exciting possibilities for violence, he volunteered for the fight against the Border Ruffians. His son John Jr. was given command of a small company of Free Staters.

The newly appointed Governor, Wilson Shannon of Cincinnati, managed to pacify the hotheads and prevent any shooting. But the bloodshed was not postponed for long. In the spring of 1856 Sheriff Jones twice went to Lawrence to enforce arrest warrants, and both times he was forcibly rebuffed. Shortly after the second attempt, he was shot and wounded in an ambush by Free State men. Soon thereafter, the Douglas County grand jury returned indictments against several Free Staters, two newspapers, and the Free State Hotel—all in Lawrence, and all charged with treason.

A federal marshal made a few arrests, but the Border Ruffians were unsatisfied. Bent on bringing the whole settlement to heel, if not to justice, they rode into Lawrence on May 21 and sacked the town. They wrecked the offending presses, bombarded the seemingly impregnable Free State Hotel with cannon and set it afire along with the Free State Governor's house. By chance, the only casualty of the drunken spree was a proslavery man killed by the collapsing hotel.

These goings-on had immediate and angry repercussions in Washington. Charles Sumner, the sonorous Senator from Massachusetts, delivered a speech he called "The Crime against Kansas," and it was one of the most violent antislavery harangues of a career noted for oratorical intemperance. The crime against Kansas, Sumner thundered, was "the rape of a virgin territory, compelling it to the hateful embrace of slavery." He reserved his harshest remarks for an aging proslavery Senator from South Carolina, Andrew P. Butler, who was absent from the Senate at the time. He ridiculed Butler's manner of speech and lambasted him for having "chosen a mistress who, though ugly to others, is always lovely to him; though polluted in the sight of the world is chaste in his sight—I mean the harlot, Slavery."

Sumner's remarks offended Southerners in general and even some of his abolitionist friends, but the angriest response came from Senator Butler's cousin, Representative Preston Brooks of South Carolina. Entering the Senate on May 22, Brooks strode up to Sumner, who was seated comfortably at his desk. Denouncing the abolitionist, Brooks brought a gutta-percha cane down on Sumner's head and continued to rain blows upon him even as the cane broke into smaller

Angry Free Staters survey the ruins of the elegant Free State Hotel, defense headquarters for the abolitionist town of Lawrence, Kansas. On May 21, 1856, proslavery Border Ruffians fired their cannon point-blank at the fortified structure, then completed their destructive handiwork by setting the hotel on fire.

and smaller pieces. It would take more than two years for the severely injured Sumner to resume his Senate seat, and until then his empty chair would remind Northerners of Southern irrationality and violence in defense of slavery. What Southerners thought of Brooks became a matter of record. He resigned his seat to permit his district to voice its opinion and was reelected almost unanimously in November 1856.

When the news of Brooks's attack on Sumner reached Kansas, John Brown was already in a dangerous mood. He had just heard of the sack of Lawrence and reportedly said to his companions, "Something must be done to show these barbarians." Sumner's caning was entirely too much for Brown; the Old Man "went crazy—*crazy*," his son Salmon reported. At Brown's command, his

sons sharpened the swords that his party was to use on May 24 at the homes of James Doyle, Allen Wilkinson and James Harris. One of Brown's neighbors urged caution. "Caution? Caution, sir?" replied Brown. "I am eternally tired of hearing that word 'caution.' It is nothing but a word of cowardice."

In choosing his victims, Brown almost certainly was thinking of more than a bloody statement of moral principle. He had some personal scores to settle as well. All of his victims, save one of Doyle's sons, were connected with the Osawatomie territorial district court—the district where John Brown lived. A month earlier, Brown's son John Jr. had been rebuffed by that court for asking incredulously whether the territory's proslavery laws would be enforced, and his subsequent declaration of resistance to the court's edicts made him guilty of contempt, an offense described as treason by the proslavery legislature. The murders of May 24 effectively removed several witnesses who could have testified against John Brown Jr.

As for the killers, there was never a question in Kansas of their identity. James Harris recognized Brown, and the widowed Mrs. Wilkinson and young John Doyle provided matching descriptions of the chief murderer. Just four days after the slaughter, enough evidence had been gathered for the sheriff to issue a warrant for Brown's arrest. Indeed, the murders so outraged frontiersmen of every stripe that even some staunch abolitionists joined with proslavery friends of the dead men to condemn the atrocity and demand that the killers be brought to justice.

But the truth about the massacre did not travel well. Within a few weeks, exaggerated and falsified reports of the killings began appearing in the Eastern press. There had been no murders at all, said one paper. Another claimed that the mutilation of the corpses proved the murders to be the work of Comanches. Some articles implied that the killings were done during a fair battle between Brown's party and proslavery men—a simple matter of self-defense. The New York *Tribune* even printed a story claiming that Brown had happened upon a band of rowdies about to do violence to a Free Stater, and that he killed the villains in the act of saving the poor antislavery man. None of those who rushed to Brown's defense seemed to notice the fact that the dead men were unarmed and murdered at their homes.

There was whitewash enough to cover Congress as well. When a Congressional committee investigated the massacre and its first witness, James Harris, began to tell

SOUTHERN CHIVALRY — ARGUMENT versus CLUB'S.

A Northern cartoon condemning South Carolina Representative Preston S. Brooks for his caning of Massachusetts Senator Charles Sumner shows Southern Senators enjoying the sight and preventing intervention by Sumner's friends. "Every Southern man sustains me," Brooks boasted in a letter to his brother. "The fragments of the stick are begged for as *sacred relics.*"

what really happened, the antislavery majority immediately cut him off and later omitted all adverse testimony from the majority report. For years, the known facts about the killings were submerged in abolitionist rhetoric. In the popular imagination of the North, the cold-blooded act became exactly what Brown had intended it to be—a righteous strike for the freedom of slaves.

In the aftermath of the Pottawatomie Massacre, John Brown lay low in his camp in the Kansas brush. For weeks the antislavery forces and the Border Ruffians postured and threatened but managed to avoid a pitched battle. A few skirmishes did take place. The largest was an attack by 250 proslavery men on Osawatomie, near where Brown and his followers were camped. One of Brown's sons was killed in the clash.

In the autumn of 1856, a newly appointed federal Governor, John W. Geary, arrived in Kansas and quickly dominated events. His policy was unprecedented in the territory: He treated Free Stater and proslavery man with the same rough justice. In the end, both factions backed down from him—and from a force of U.S. Army troops who brooked no nonsense from either side. At last, a troubled quiet settled on the plains. Both sides returned to the business of gobbling up and profiting from the land. Old opponents often were seen working together. The New York press soon commented that "the love of the almighty dollar had melted away the iron of bitterness and Anti-Slavery and Pro-Slavery men were standing together as a unit on their rights as squatters."

The whole nation seemed to heave a great sigh of relief as the crisis in Kansas cooled. The disunion talk—or at least most of it—had subsided. Yet the quiet was bound to be short-lived, for in March of 1857 the Supreme Court was to announce its verdict in a case that supposedly would settle the precise legal status of slavery in the territories.

The case in question went back almost two decades—to a time when the Missouri Compromise, with its ban of slavery in territories north of 36° 30′, was still the law of the land. At stake was the status of an elderly black man named Dred Scott. In 1834 Scott's owner—an Army surgeon named John Emerson—took his slave from Missouri to a military post in Illinois, though slavery was outlawed in that state. Two years later, transferred to another post, Emerson took Scott to the Wisconsin Territory, where slavery was also outlawed. Emerson eventually brought Scott back to Missouri, where the surgeon died in 1843.

Three years later Scott, with the help of local antislavery lawyers, sued Emerson's heirs for his freedom, contending that his years in Illinois and Wisconsin had made him free. Scott lost his case, then won on appeal in 1850, only to see the Missouri state supreme court reverse the appeal and once again consign him to slavery. Scott thereupon took his case to the federal courts, where he lost again in 1854. After another two years the U.S. Supreme Court agreed to hear the case.

The two key questions posed by the case were prickly. First, was Scott a citizen with the right to sue in the federal courts? Second, was he free as a result of having lived in the Wisconsin Territory, where slavery was outlawed by the Missouri Compromise? Moreover, the second question patently involved the constitutionality of the Missouri Compromise's prohibition of slavery. Did Con-

Chief Justice Roger Taney, the wealthy Marylander who handed down the Supreme Court's proslavery decision in the Dred Scott case, personally deplored slavery and had even freed his own bondsmen.

gress really have the power to regulate slavery in the territories?

Chief Justice Roger B. Taney, the 79-year-old scion of a wealthy, slave-owning Maryland family, announced the Court's decision on March 6. As to Scott's right to sue, Taney held that he had none: Slaves and freed descendants of slaves were not citizens, said Taney, because at the time the Constitution was written, blacks "had for more than a century been regarded as beings of an inferior order . . . so far inferior that they had no rights which the white man was bound to respect." As to Scott's freedom, Taney held that he had none of that either: Slaves were property, and slaveholders had an absolute right to take their property with them into the territories. The Fifth Amendment guaranteed that no person should "be deprived of life, liberty or property without due process

of law." Any law, said Taney, that abridged such a constitutionally protected right was in itself a violation of due process. In other words, Congress had violated the Constitution in enacting the Missouri Compromise. Dred Scott had lost on all counts.

The reaction was immediate. Proslavery people hailed the decision as the final vindication of their rights. From the antislavery states came cries of outrage. The Dred Scott ruling had come from a Supreme Court dominated by Southerners, rekindling fears of a "slave power" conspiracy in the federal government—a plot by a wealthy, cruel minority to thwart democratic rule by the majority. The attack on the Court was venomous. Chief Justice Taney was vilified for his "wicked and false judgment," for his "gross historical falsehoods," and for his "jesuitical decision"—a slurring reference to his Roman Catholic faith. "If epithets and denunciations could sink a judicial-body," said one observer, "the Supreme Court of the United States would never be heard from again."

And so the South had gained another victory. Yet the Southern triumphs in the controversy over the Fugitive Slave Law, the Missouri Compromise repeal, the crooked Kansas legislature and now the Dred Scott decision brought the South closer and closer to defeat, for each victory made old enemies stronger and added new enemies to the ranks of hard-line abolitionists and emancipationists. And by 1857, more pyrrhic victories were in the offing for the South and more enemies were about to be made. For Kansas was ready to bleed again.

Shortly before Democrat James Buchanan became President in 1857, the proslavery Kansas legislature started a drive for state-

Dred Scott, the slave who sue his freedom on the groun his master had transported h a territory where slaver prohibited, was the subject of page stories like this one for m after the Supreme Court against him in March 1857. But won out in spite of the court deci He, his wife and their two daug were freed by a new ma

FRANK LESLIE'S
ILLUSTRATED

NEWSPAPER

Entered according to Act of Congress, in the year 1857, by FRANK LESLIE, in the Clerk's Office of the District Court for the Southern District of New York. (Copyrighted June 22, 1857.)

No. 82.—VOL. IV.]   NEW YORK, SATURDAY, JUNE 27, 1857.   [PRICE 6 CENTS.

TO TOURISTS AND TRAVELLERS.

We shall be happy to receive personal narratives, of land or sea, including adventures and incidents, from every person who pleases to correspond with our paper.

We take this opportunity of returning our thanks to our numerous artistic correspondents throughout the country, for the many sketches we are constantly receiving from them of the news of the day. We trust they will spare no pains to furnish us with drawings of events as they may occur. We would also remind them that it is necessary to send all sketches, if possible, by the earliest conveyance.

VISIT TO DRED SCOTT—HIS FAMILY—INCIDENTS OF HIS LIFE—DECISION OF THE SUPREME COURT.

WHILE standing in the Fair grounds at St. Louis, and engaged in conversation with a prominent citizen of that enterprising city, he suddenly asked us if we would not like to be introduced to Dred Scott. Upon expressing a desire to be thus honored, the gentleman called to an old negro who was standing near by, and our wish was gratified. Dred made a rude, obeisance to our recognition, and seemed to enjoy the notice we expended upon him. We found him on examination to be a pure-blooded African, perhaps fifty years of age, with a shrewd, intelligent, good-natured face, of rather light frame, being not more than five feet six inches high. After some general remarks we expressed a wish to get his portrait (we had made

ELIZA AND LIZZIE, CHILDREN OF DRED SCOTT.

efforts before, through correspondents, and failed), and asked him if he would not go to Fitzgibbon's gallery and

have it taken. The gentleman present explained to Dred that it was proper he should have his likeness in the "great illustrated paper of the country," overruled his many objections, which seemed to grow out of a superstitious feeling, and he promised to be at the gallery the next day. This appointment Dred did not keep. Determined not to be foiled, we sought an interview with Mr. Crane, Dred's lawyer, who promptly gave us a letter of introduction, explaining to Dred that it was to his advantage to have his picture taken to be engraved for our paper, and also directions where we could find his domicile. We found the place with difficulty, the streets in Dred's neighborhood being more clearly defined in the plan of the city than on the mother earth; we finally reached a wooden house, however, protected by a balcony that answered the description. Approaching the door, we saw a smart, tidy-looking negress, perhaps thirty years of age, who, with two female assistants, was busy ironing. To our question, "Is this where Dred Scott lives?" we received, rather hesitatingly, the answer, "Yes." Upon our asking if he was home, she said,

"What white man arter dad nigger for?—why don't white man 'tend to his own business, and let dat nigger 'lone? Some of dese days dey'll steal dat nigger—dat are a fact."

DRED SCOTT. PHOTOGRAPHED BY FITZGIBBON, OF ST. LOUIS.

HIS WIFE, HARRIET. PHOTOGRAPHED BY FITZGIBBON, OF ST. LOUIS.

hood. As President, Buchanan encouraged the movement, hoping to sweep Kansas into the Union as a Democratic state. His hand-picked new Governor, a 110-pound bantam rooster named Robert J. Walker, tried his best to get a hold on the situation. But both Walker and the President misjudged the depth and bitterness of the divisions that racked the territory.

Further, Buchanan underestimated the chances for error in the normal process by which a territory became a state. A census of the territory had to be taken so that district lines could be laid out and delegates elected to a constitutional convention. The convention, in turn, would determine how slavery would be handled in the constitution of the new state. And as usual in Kansas, everything that could go wrong would go wrong.

Quite reasonably, the Kansas Free Staters assumed that the census and the ensuing election of convention delegates would be fraudulent, like everything else that had been administered by Kansas' proslavery forces. Their assumption was on the mark. Proslavery officials gerrymandered the election districts so that proslavery counties were certain to control the constitutional convention. Consequently, Free State voters boycotted the election, and when convention delegates met in the autumn of 1857 at Lecompton, the territorial capital, they were an all-proslavery fraternity.

Meanwhile, the regularly scheduled election for a new Kansas legislature had taken place. Free Staters had recently been pouring into the territory, and assurances by the territorial governor that the election would be fair brought them to the polls. Outnumbering proslavery settlers by almost 2 to 1, they won control of the legislature. Kansas now had a legally chosen antislavery legislature and a legally chosen proslavery constitutional convention. Of course the two were bound to clash.

The convention quickly passed a constitution that was essentially proslavery. However, knowing that the document would have to stand the test of a general referendum, the delegates adopted an alternate strategy. They drafted an article that guaranteed a slaveholder's right to retain title to slaves then living in the territory and to their direct descendants, but that outlawed the importation of any more slaves. Taking remarkable liberties with the English language, they called their new document the constitution "without slavery." Voters were to be given a choice between the new document and the original provision—the constitution "with slavery"—which allowed the future importation of slaves.

Free State men, recognizing the referendum as a farce, boycotted it, and on December 21 the Lecompton Constitution passed "with slavery." Thereupon the antislavery legislature pushed through a law that would put the entire Lecompton Constitution, not just the slavery question, to a popular vote. On January 4, 1858, only 14 days after it had passed "with slavery," the constitution was roundly defeated in a vote that the proslavery men now boycotted. For the third time, Kansas saw an election in which one side or the other declined to participate.

And now President Buchanan stepped in with his customary lack of sagacity. He saw himself as a "pacificator," a man who would settle these annoying problems once and for all. He declared the rejection of the constitution invalid, and recommended that Congress admit Kansas as a state on the basis of

A Republican cartoon, published during the presidential campaign of 1856, attacks the Democrats for favoring a popular vote to decide the status of slavery in Kansas, implying (correctly, as it turned out) that stuffed ballot boxes would force the Free Staters to swallow slavery. Even though Kansas remained open to slavery, the territory was so poorly suited to slave-grown crops that in 1860 it had only two slaves.

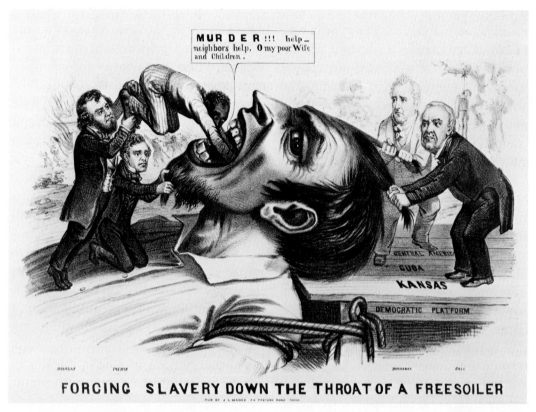

MURDER !!! help— neighbors help, O my poor Wife and Children.

DOUGLAS   PIERCE   BUCHANAN   CASS

FORCING SLAVERY DOWN THE THROAT OF A FREESOILER

the Lecompton Constitution "with slavery." If Congress accepted his wishes, he avowed, the Union would at last have "domestic peace" on the Kansas question.

Instead of bringing peace, Buchanan's proposals raised hob. His fellow Democrat Stephen Douglas broke with him over the Lecompton mess, as did many others in the party. Some Northern and most Western Democrats sided with Douglas; Southerners went down the line with Buchanan. Despite the breaches of party loyalty, Buchanan still could marshal a majority in the Senate, where he got a victory in late March. The House was another matter, however, and Buchanan made matters worse by rejecting compromise. The bill must go through "naked," he said.

Buchanan's obstinance doomed the mea-

sure, and it was defeated in the House on April 1. Yet finally a compromise of sorts was worked out. Congress would resubmit the constitution to the voters of Kansas along with a thinly veiled threat. They could vote on the whole constitution. If they accepted it, Kansas would be a slave state. If they rejected it, then Kansas could not reapply for statehood for several years, until the population rose to the 90,000 mark.

Kansas did reject it overwhelmingly. That was the end of the Lecompton Constitution. And, since the Free Staters were increasingly in control, that was the end of nearly five years of strife in and over Kansas.

In that time the Democratic Party had been fatally split and the Republican Party was born. In the deepening crisis the nation had been left with a single, bitter political alignment—North against South. States-manship had disappeared. The press in both the North and the South carried inflammatory rhetoric to new heights of passion, new depths of unreasoned partisanship. The North feared a conspiracy by the slaveholders. The South feared an increasingly enraged North and an ever more powerful antislavery force in Congress.

The reaction to these fears was dramatic. In the streets of every big city in the North, in the park lands and parade grounds of the South, fraternal and recreational militia companies were being mustered and drilled. There was no hostile intent, the organizers claimed. But there was a martial spirit in the air. Everyone loved the gay uniforms, the fancy precision marching, the ideal of competition exemplified in contests between drill teams.

But in the hills of Western Maryland a private citizen was raising his own special kind of militia with intentions that were intensely and undisguisedly hostile. John Brown had come there to pay a call on Harpers Ferry, a town just across the Maryland line, in Virginia (later West Virginia).

Although Brown had controlled his thirst for blood in the months after the Pottawatomie Massacre, he was anything but inactive. He was now a full-time worker for emancipation, and he nurtured a grandiose plan for a death blow against slavery. To realize his dream he would need money to equip a small army. For that he first procured letters of recommendation from the current Free State "governor" of Kansas, Charles Robinson, and then launched himself on an ambitious fund-raising tour.

For two and a half years, between January 1857 and July 1859, Brown shuttled back and forth between Kansas and the Northeast, principally Boston, where he was welcomed into the salons of the country's most prominent abolitionists. Among those who contributed small sums of money were Gerrit Smith, Thomas Wentworth Higginson, Theodore Parker and Amos Lawrence, the man for whom Lawrence, Kansas, was named—four of the most influential antislavery men in the Northeast. Brown visited Senator Charles Sumner, who was still recuperating from his caning by South Carolina's Preston Brooks. The Old Man asked to see the bloodstained coat Sumner had worn the day of the attack. Handed the sanctified garment, Brown fell silent and, recalled Sumner, "his lips compressed and his eyes shone like polished steel."

The money Brown raised in the Northeast turned out to be a mere pittance; it bought equipment and supplies for a tiny band of soldiers—barely more than a dozen followers, among them four of his sons. He also hired an English mercenary, Hugh Forbes, to act as military adviser and drillmaster for his minuscule legion. Then he commissioned the manufacture of 1,000 long pikes, for what purpose he did not reveal. Indeed, Brown revealed little of his vague plans to anyone.

By the beginning of 1858, however, his strategy had jelled somewhat. Kansas was no longer a satisfactory arena for the Lord's revenge against slaveowners; the Free Staters were clearly winning command. He and his men must take their crusade elsewhere. So he dismissed them for a while and told them to rendezvous in Tabor, Iowa, where they would drill and he would reveal to them his wondrous plans for the future. Only nine recruits showed up in Tabor. Undismayed by the poor turnout, Brown announced, "Our ultimate destination is Virginia."

Brown had long harbored the notion of setting up a base in the Alleghenies from which he could invade Virginia, liberate many slaves and bring them back into the mountain fastnesses. There he would train the freed blacks and lead them on a larger raid that would, he thought, foment a general slave insurrection in Virginia. Eventually he and his army of rebels would take over a substantial piece of territory in the South, forming a kind of black state in which he would confiscate the land of slaveholders, proclaim martial law and exercise his own form of government.

All this Brown made clear in a "constitution" that he drew up in January 1858. He discussed his wild plan with some backers in the East, and some of them tried to discourage him. But a few—the men who would come to be known to Brown and to one another as the Secret Six—agreed to provide him with funds. Besides Smith, Higginson and Parker, the six included George L. Stearns, Franklin B. Sanborn and Samuel Gridley Howe—all well-connected leaders of their Northeastern communities.

At first, Brown was apparently reluctant to inform the Secret Six of the precise time and place of his initial strike. He did tell the mercenary Hugh Forbes that his intention was to stage an arms-stealing raid on the U.S. arsenal at Harpers Ferry. And in May of 1858, Forbes, angry because Brown had failed to pay him, disclosed the plan to two abolitionist Senators—Henry Wilson of Massachusetts and William H. Seward of New York. The legislators kept the secret, but they berated the Secret Six for their in-

volvement in such a harebrained scheme. Thereupon, the six told Brown to stop, urged him to go back to Kansas to cover his tracks, and further declared that henceforth Brown was not to reveal any of his intentions to them. What they really meant was quite simple: They still wanted him to strike a blow, but they did not want to know anything that might be damaging to them. Brown lamented that his backers "were not men of action."

Ostensibly chastened but fundamentally undeterred, Brown went back to Kansas in mid-1858 and, adopting the pseudonym Shubel Morgan, soon led a successful foray into Missouri and freed 11 slaves, two of whom joined his band. For months he was constantly on the go. Then, in July 1859, he journeyed to Maryland and rented a farm just to the north of Harpers Ferry. There he made his final plans and passed the summer trying to raise more men and money.

By October the pikes had arrived, several hundred guns were ready, and friends assured Brown that the slaves in Virginia were eager to join him. His 21 men grew restless; they worried about being betrayed, for dozens of people now knew of their intentions. In fact, John B. Floyd, Buchanan's pro-Southern Secretary of War, had been warned of the guerrilla raid, but he dismissed the story as ludicrous.

Yet Brown, for all his grand plans, had overlooked the details on which the attack would hinge. He made no careful reconnaissance of Harpers Ferry, no effort to alert the Virginia slaves, no plans for emergencies in case his attack went awry. All would go flawlessly, he believed, because God was on his side. And so he would wait no more. Late on October 16, 1859, John Brown and his army

The federal armory at Harpers Ferry (below) contained the guns and ammunition that John Brown and his men needed to foment a slave uprising. But less than 36 hours after the raiders took over, U.S. Marines commanded by Lieutenant Colonel Robert E. Lee stormed the fire-engine house just inside the armory gate (left), taking Brown prisoner.

of 16 whites, four free blacks and one escaped slave were primed for their great mission. "Men, get on your arms," he said to them. "We will proceed to the Ferry."

Brown led the party through a cold drizzle—he in a wagon, his men hiking behind him, their rifles hidden under gray woolen shawls. Soon they were crossing the Potomac River on a covered bridge that took them directly into Harpers Ferry. Brown posted two guards on that bridge and sent sentries to the other bridge leading into town. Then the party moved toward the U.S. arsenal on Potomac Street.

It all went with remarkable ease. The watchman at the arsenal was taken by surprise. Brown told him: "I came here from Kansas, and this is a slave State; I want to free all the Negroes in this State; I have possession now of the United States armory, and if the citizens interfere with me I must only burn the town and have blood."

Soon afterward the raiders captured the nearby Hall's Rifle Works. Next, Brown sent a few of his men to seize some prominent hostages, particularly Colonel Lewis Washington, a prosperous slaveowner and a great-grandnephew of the first President. Following explicit instructions from Brown, the contingent brought back not only Colonel Washington but also a sword belonging to him that tradition said had been presented to George Washington by Frederick the Great. Brown strapped the weapon around his waist and waited, expecting slaves by the thousands to rally to him. Once he had armed them from the arsenal, they would march on in his campaign of liberation.

The slaves did not come, and Brown's plan began to fall apart. An eastbound train was stopped at the bridge and the engineer was warned to back away. One of Brown's men shot and mortally wounded a railroad baggageman near the bridge. The victim was a free black.

The town was thoroughly aroused by now, and before long, telegraph wires all over the East hummed with exaggerated reports of "Negro insurrection at Harper's Ferry! Fire and Rapine on the Virginia Border!" In the nearby Virginia countryside, several militia companies formed up and headed for the town. They arrived on October 17 and found the townsmen and Brown's raiders in a blistering exchange of fire.

The raiders were pinned down in the armory buildings and in Hall's Rifle Works, under a constant fire from positions in the town. John Brown was paralyzed by indecision; not knowing what to do next, he did nothing. After four hours of battle the raiders suffered their first casualty. Dangerfield Newby, a black, was killed. Townspeople dragged his body to a gutter and cut off his ears and let hogs chew on the corpse. Clearly, the raiders could expect no mercy from the townsmen, whose heavy drinking only added to their savagery.

Faced with a siege, Brown withdrew most of his men to the fire-engine house adjacent to the armory and there barricaded himself with his hostages. Soon after 1 p.m. he sent two men out to negotiate under a truce flag. They were shot down. One of them, his son Watson, struggled back to the engine house in agony.

The battle went on all afternoon. When a raider tried to flee, townsmen shot him to death and for hours used his body for target practice. Three of Brown's men were driven out of Hall's Rifle Works. One was killed outright, one mortally wounded in a cross

fire, and the third was taken prisoner and nearly lynched before a local physician rescued him. In the melee the mayor of Harpers Ferry was shot dead. Drunken townsmen took revenge at about 4 p.m. They hauled out a raider whom they had captured that morning, killed him in cold blood and used his body, too, for target practice.

Brown tried yet again to parley, offering to release his hostages if he and his 14 remaining men were allowed to leave. No deal could be made. The raiders spent a cold, hungry night in the engine house, listening to desultory gunfire and a drunken ruckus in the town. By then, Brown's son Oliver had been wounded, and he lay beside brother Watson, both of them dying in vivid pain. Oliver begged his father to kill him and end his misery. "If you must die, die like a man," Brown replied in cold anger. Some time later he called to Oliver and got no reply. "I guess he is dead," said John Brown.

The next morning Brown looked out of his "fort" at 2,000 hostile people, including a company of Marines newly arrived from Washington. The Marines were armed with muskets, fixed bayonets and sledge hammers, and were preparing to storm the engine house. Their commander was Lieutenant Colonel Robert E. Lee of the 2nd United States Cavalry. Lee sent Lieutenant James Ewell Brown (Jeb) Stuart forward under a white flag to demand surrender and promise protection for the raiders.

Brown met Stuart at the door and made impossible counterproposals to the surrender ultimatum. Thereupon Stuart jumped aside and waved his hat as a signal for the Marines to charge. They battered through a door and killed two raiders with the bayonets. A hostage pointed out Brown to the

Lieutenant Colonel Robert E. Lee was home on leave in Arlington, Virginia, when he was called to put down an insurrection at Harpers Ferry—actually, John Brown's raid. Lee hurried off without donning a uniform; he commanded the Marine assault force in civilian dress.

Lieutenant James Ewell Brown (Jeb) Stuart of the 1st U.S. Cavalry journeyed to Harpers Ferry as Lee's aide. There, he distinguished himself by carrying Lee's surrender demand to John Brown—an act that foreshadowed his gallantry as a Confederate cavalry commander.

troops, and a lieutenant bludgeoned him to the ground with his blunt sword.

With that, the Marine assault ended abruptly. Of the 21 raiders who had come to Harpers Ferry with Brown, only he and four others remained. Ten were dead or dying, and the rest had fled, though two would be captured later. Four civilians and one Marine also were dead, along with two slaves who had answered Brown's call to arms.

News of the raid electrified the nation. Almost without exception, Southern whites were frightened. Many of them accused the North in general and the Republicans in particular of a plot to subdue the South with a gigantic slave rebellion. "Yea, a servile war with all its untold horror," a South Carolina legislator declaimed, and a South Carolina militiaman harped on the South's constant racist fear of "mongrel tyrants who mean to reduce you and your wives and your daughters on a level with the very slaves you buy and sell." Confronted with this sort of poisonous invective, the Republicans tried to dissociate themselves from Brown, and some even hoped that the Old Man would be tried and hanged quickly to spare them further embarrassment.

The trial of Brown and his fellow captives, conducted by the state of Virginia, did begin quickly, just 10 days after the raid. The injured Old Man was carried into the courtroom at Charles Town, Virginia; he lay on a cot through the week-long trial. He was skillfully defended, and spoke eloquently in his own behalf, but the verdict was never in doubt: John Brown and his raiders must hang for murder and treason.

During the trial and the wait for execution, Brown won no little admiration for his dignity, his iron will, his implacable commitment to his ideals. Archsecessionist Edmund Ruffin said, as one fanatic of another: "It is impossible for me not to respect his thorough devotion to his bad cause, and the undaunted courage with which he has sustained it, through all losses and hazards."

Another agitator, the noted abolitionist Reverend Henry Ward Beecher, understood that John Brown would soon render his greatest service to his cause. "Let Virginia make him a martyr!" he cried. "Now, he has only blundered. His soul was noble; his work miserable. But a cord and a gibbet would redeem all that, and round up Brown's failure with a heroic success."

Brown himself wanted martyrdom and claimed it, delivering, on the occasion of his sentencing, a speech that instantly became a revered classic in the North. Said he: "I believe that to have interfered as I have done, as I have always freely admitted I have done, in behalf of His despised poor, is no wrong, but right. Now, if it is deemed necessary that I should forfeit my life for the furtherance of the ends of justice, and mingle my blood further with the blood of my children and with the blood of millions in this slave country whose rights are disregarded by wicked, cruel, and unjust enactments, I say, let it be done."

John Brown uttered no last words on the scaffold. But on the way to his execution on a December day in 1859 he handed a guard a final note that exactly predicted the national calamity he had done so much to make inevitable. "I John Brown," the message said, "am now quite certain that the crimes of this guilty land will never be purged away but with blood."

John Brown's Body

John Brown was a dead man. So Brown himself realized on October 18, 1859, even as federal troops crushed his 22-man raid on Harpers Ferry; his attempt to start a great slave revolution in Virginia had ended with 17 people killed, and it would lead to his execution for conspiracy, treason and murder. In fact, the bloodstained fanatic was to be hurried to his death just 45 days hence.

The rush to hang him was not vindictive. Local officials felt that if the law moved too slowly, Brown might be lynched by outraged Southerners. So on the 19th of October, the "Old Man," weakened by injuries he had suffered during his capture, was whisked off to stand trial in Charles Town, Virginia (later West Virginia). He was carried into the courtroom and deposited on a cot. Despite his lawyers' urging, he refused to demean himself by pleading insanity. "Not guilty," said Brown, which was exactly how he felt.

It took three days for the lawyers to have their say. Then it took barely 45 minutes for the jury to hand down the verdict. Brown showed not a flicker of emotion as Judge Richard Parker sentenced him to hang.

During his last month, Brown was allowed to receive visitors in his cell and to write farewell letters to supporters. In a note to his brother, he accurately appraised his fate: "I am worth inconceivably more to hang than for any other purpose."

Such was his victory. On December 2, John Brown mounted the gallows and went calmly to his death, inspiring countless others to press his crusade to free the slaves. Not long afterward, as Yankee soldiers marched off to fight the Confederates, they would sing: "John Brown's body lies a'mouldering in the grave. . . ."

Rifle in hand, old John Brown holds a hostage at bay shortly before U.S. Marines broke into the Harpers Ferry arsenal and clubbed him down. Two of Brown's raiders keep up their musket fire; another lies wounded at his feet.

Lying injured after the battle, Brown tells his captors, "I acknowledge no master in human form." Among his visitors was Virginia Governor Henry A. Wise.

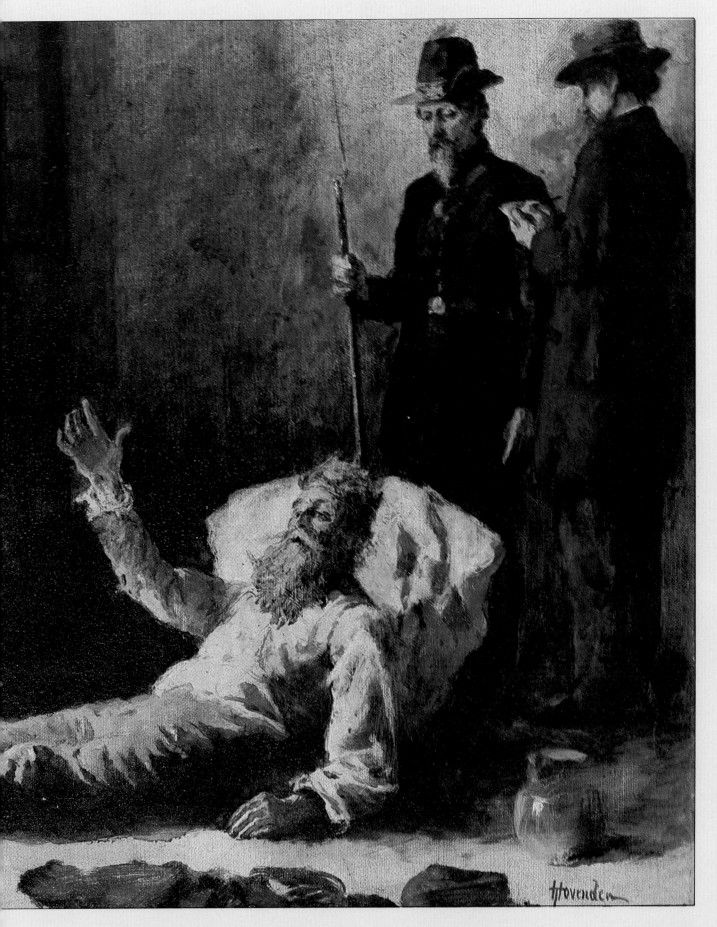

Lifted from his cot and supported by deputies, John Brown makes a statement shortly before Judge Richard Parker *(left)* sentences him to hang. Brown informed the hushed courtroom, "I feel no consciousness of guilt."

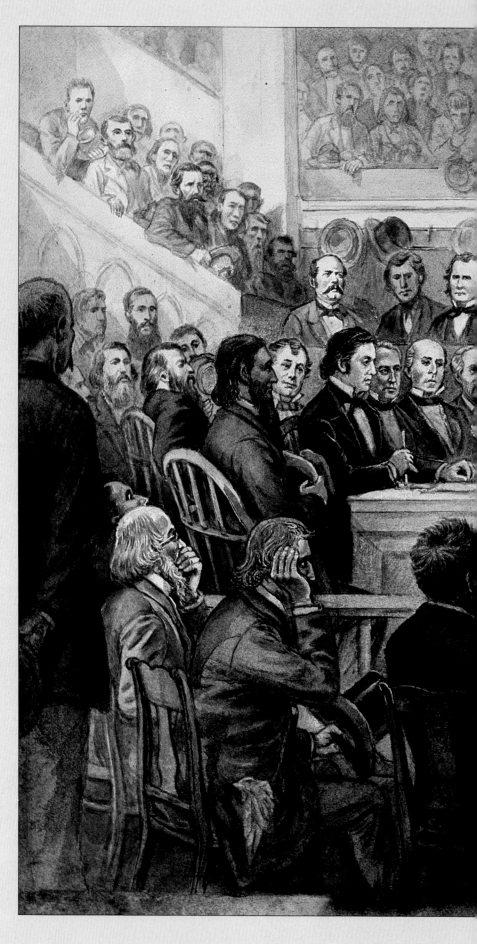

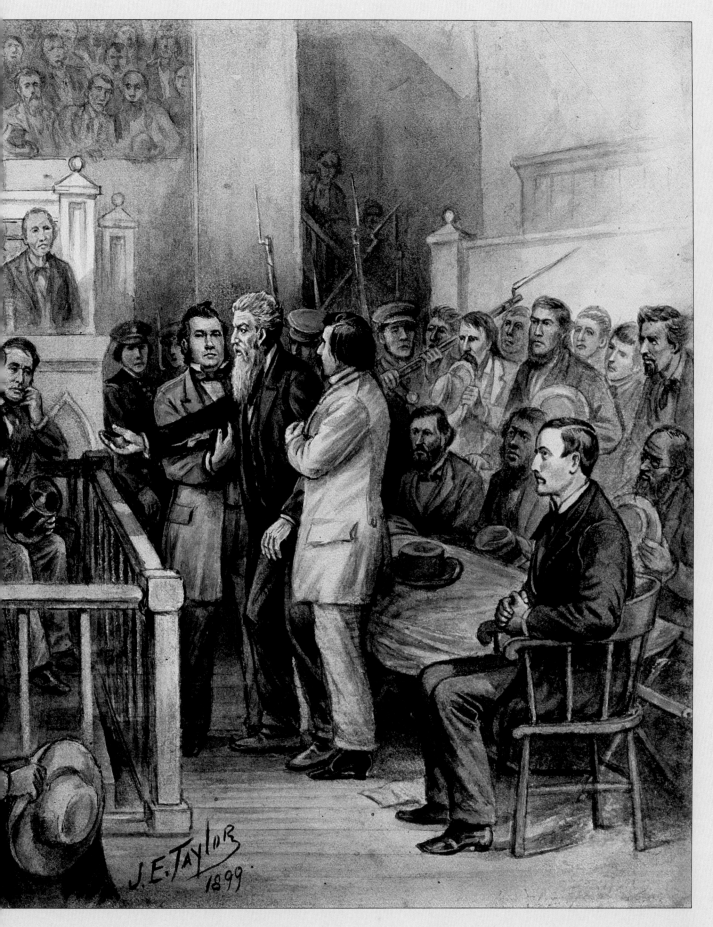

J.E.Taylor
1899.

A guard of 1,500 troops looks on as John Brown's body swings from a gallows outside Charles Town. The witnesses included actor John Wilkes Booth

...ofessor at the Virginia Military Institute in Lexington—Thomas J. Jackson (later called Stonewall).

Lincoln of Illinois

On the evening of February 27, 1860, some 1,500 New Yorkers braved a snowstorm to hear Abraham Lincoln, a little-known Illinois politician, speak at Cooper Union, an institution of free instruction in the arts and applied sciences. Lincoln was to discuss the cruel problems facing the nation, and inevitably the central issue would be slavery and its future in America.

The tall Westerner would be addressing the cream of New York's intellectual and political society, leaders and opinion makers who surely would influence, for good or for ill, Lincoln's chances for the Republican presidential nomination. This was not the sort of group that a partisan stump speech could rouse to fever pitch; closely reasoned arguments rather than passion were clearly called for. If the outlander could move the gathering merely to judicious applause, then he would have gone some distance toward the prize he ardently sought.

Lincoln had his doubts about whether he was up to the task. These well-to-do sophisticates might snicker at his rude, rural twang, at the ill-fitting suit stretched over his lanky frame. They might follow their Eastern prejudices against men of the West and refuse to hearken to his words. But Lincoln had suffered snobbery before and he had not been stopped by it.

As his topic, Lincoln chose to discuss the question of whether the federal government had the Constitutional right to control the extension of black servitude to the territories. Three years before, the Supreme Court had ruled in the Dred Scott decision that Congress lacked that power, setting off a tumult of protest in the Northern states and rallying to the antislavery cause countless people who had previously been content to ignore the issue. Now, at Cooper Union, Lincoln argued that the Supreme Court decision was wrong.

If Lincoln was nervous when he began his speech, his unease quickly vanished; he warmed to his subject and the audience warmed to him. Citing the voting records of the Founding Fathers in Congress and in various pre-Constitutional conventions, he established that they had voted routinely on proposals to extend slavery to the old Northwest Territory and, later, the Louisiana Territory. Lincoln declared that even though the Constitution did not specifically forbid or endorse the extension of slavery, the framers of the Constitution had always acted on the assumption that Congress would rule on the slavery question on a case-by-case basis. The Supreme Court, in sum, had failed to take into account the obvious intent of the framers of the Constitution. Having drawn this conclusion, Lincoln used it to rebut the Southern charge that the Republicans were wild-eyed radicals. They were no more radical, he said, than the Founding Fathers.

Then Lincoln turned his attention to slavery as a moral issue. Here he found himself caught in a contradiction. On the one hand, he said, neither he nor the Republican Party

Wooden statuettes carved by contemporary folk artists represent Stephen A. Douglas (*top*) and Abraham Lincoln, political archrivals whose spirited contests for the Senate and the Presidency riveted the nation in the years before the War.

sought to interfere with slavery in those states where it then existed. On the other, slavery was, in his view, a dreadful wrong, a denial of the American principle that all men are created equal. The South, he declared, would be satisfied only when the free states recognized slavery as being right. "Can we," Lincoln asked, "cast our votes with their view, and against our own? . . . If our sense of duty forbids this, then let us stand by our duty fearlessly and effectively. . . . Let us have faith that right makes might, and in that faith, let us, to the end, dare to do our duty as we understand it."

Thus, Abraham Lincoln was challenging not only the South but his own political party as well. When he ended, his listeners rose as one; many cheered immoderately. The man from Illinois had deeply impressed this powerful group. He was not yet their choice as candidate, but that night he had emerged as a major contender for the honor and the travail. Later, after his election, Lincoln remarked that this speech more than any other had brought him the Republican presidential nomination.

Perhaps only in an overheated political climate could a man like Lincoln have vaulted to prominence. True, he was little known in the East before the Cooper Union speech, but he was hardly obscure. Two years before, he had startled the nation when his attempt to unseat Stephen A. Douglas, the powerful Democratic Senator from Illinois, had come within a hairbreadth of success. In his home state, he was already something of a legend. Tales of his obscure Kentucky birth in 1809, his hardscrabble childhood on the Indiana and Illinois frontiers, and his young manhood splitting rails and studying

for the bar had circulated widely. His own summation of his youthful years was a line from Thomas Gray's "Elegy Written in a Country Churchyard": "The short and simple annals of the poor."

Yet there was nothing simple about Abraham Lincoln. Wit, drive, intelligence and years of experience as a country lawyer had made him a masterly politician. He had gone on to serve four terms in the state legislature and one in Congress. From his office in Springfield, Lincoln had become one of the state's chief political wire pullers, first in the service of the Whigs, then for the Republicans. He enjoyed a perception more acute than most men and an unequaled power to express it. He could speak compellingly in the idioms of coarse country humor or a rolling rhetoric he had learned from reading Shakespeare and the Bible.

His antislavery sentiments reflected the complicated yet practical cast of his mind. Though he loathed slavery unequivocally, he was not a doctrinaire abolitionist. As a lawyer, he had no difficulty representing a slaveholder seeking the return of a fugitive slave. And in the 1850s he refused to join the clamor for the early emancipation of blacks. For the short run, he was willing to tolerate slavery in those states where the institution already existed. But he staunchly opposed its extension to new territories, believing that this would saddle the Union with a system that was both evil and economically retrograde. If contained, slavery might be eradicated in time through peaceful means; if allowed to spread, it would undermine free labor, retard economic development and, inevitably, destroy the democratic basis on which the nation was built. Now, in early 1860, Lincoln—though neither he nor any-

AN AMALGAMATION POLKA.

Blacks and whites dance together in an 1845 cartoon lambasting a Boston clergyman who declared that the "blending of the two races by amalgamation is just what is needed for the perfection of both." Proponents of race-mixing were few, but Southerners called the abolitionists "amalgamators" for urging that blacks be absorbed into white society on an equal footing.

one else knew it—stood atop the shambles of a political-party system that had been falling apart for at least eight years. A new America waited to be born, and Abraham Lincoln would be its progenitor.

The disintegration of the old regime had begun in 1852, when Young America—a faction of the Democratic Party that wanted to pry control from the hands of the "old fogies" who had been running things for years—failed to gain the presidential nomination for its candidate, Stephen Douglas. Instead, the Democrats' nod went to a former general and undistinguished Congressman named Franklin Pierce, a Northerner with Southern views. After Pierce's nomination and election, the Young America organization withered, and its exuberant nationalism was replaced by the sinister forces of nativism and resurgent sectionalism.

In spite of the stated American ideals of religious and social tolerance, the country had always displayed a strain of prejudice. During the early 1850s it grew more pronounced, with many native-born Americans turning against foreigners and many Protestants turning against Catholics. The cause or excuse was, quite simply, the great increase in the number of people arriving from famine-stricken Ireland and from the German states, where liberal revolutions had been crushed in the 1840s. Hundreds of thousands of German and Irish immigrants swelled the populations of East Coast cities and moved west into the Mississippi Valley and the states and territories around the Great Lakes. They vied with the native-born for jobs and land. Moreover, if they were Catholics, their loyalty to the United States was feared to be secondary to their obedience to the Pope in Rome. The members of the aristocratic, puritanical Whig Party, which was slowly breaking up into contentious splinter groups, discerned yet another detestable quality in the immigrants: Almost invariably, they joined the Democratic Party, which traditionally campaigned for the welfare of the ordinary citizen.

In reaction, a new party evolved. Under the banner of the American Party, thousands of disillusioned Whigs and Democrats turned to nativism, convened in secret, developed all manner of clandestine signals and signs, and dedicated themselves to restricting the political power of immigrants. When questioned by outsiders, the nativists denied all knowledge of the new movement or anything related to it, prompting New York *Tribune* editor Horace Greeley to label them the "Know-Nothings."

In the four years following the election of Franklin Pierce, the Know-Nothing movement seemed irresistible, with its candidates in local and statewide elections capturing much of New England, New York and Pennsylvania and making inroads into the Upper South. Yet most old-line Whigs resisted the xenophobic tide. In Illinois, Abraham Lincoln, then still a Whig, loathed the Know-Nothings and wrote that if they came to power, the Declaration of Independence would have to be changed to read, " 'All men are created equal,' except negroes, and foreigners and catholics."

By 1856, the Know-Nothing madness had begun to recede: The Kansas issue had once again brought the sectional controversy to the fore. In the meantime, thousands of Northern Whigs were joining the burgeoning Republican Party.

Tradition has it that the Republican Party was born on February 28, 1854, in the small Wisconsin town of Ripon, when a group of Whigs, Free Soilers (members of a splinter party opposed to the extension of slavery) and Democrats met to express their outrage over Stephen Douglas' recently introduced Kansas-Nebraska bill. Actually, many such groups sprang up independently at the time, all of them eager to establish a new party capable of uniting the various antislavery factions under a single banner. The Ripon meeting adopted a motion that this movement call itself Republican. The name was a logical choice, harking back to two mainstreams in the American political legacy: Thomas Jefferson's Democratic-Republican Party, the institutional expression of the equality of man; and John Quincy Adams' and Henry Clay's National Republicans, the precursors of the Whigs and proponents of a strong central government.

From the outset, the Republicans were a sectional party—but theirs was a mighty section. They drew their support entirely from the North and the West, which possessed much of the nation's food supply, most of its population, most of its industry, most of its commerce and most of its railroads. The Republicans could afford to lose the entire South and all of the border states and still win national power. The time was approaching when it would be possible to bind the North and West together in a grand coalition of disappointed Whigs, frustrated Free Soilers, disaffected Democrats and reformed Know-Nothings to oppose the extension of slavery—and, ultimately, slavery's very existence.

Still, it was no easy matter for an active partisan to cast off loyalty to an old party, even if it was moribund. Lincoln, who was then engaged in the private practice of law in Springfield, shunned the new Republicans at first, fearing that he would be associated with the radical abolitionists. As late as August of 1855, he confessed that he was uncertain where his loyalties lay, but "I think I am a Whig," he wrote. By the end of that year, Lincoln had moved closer to the Republicans, seeking a working relationship with those he had once considered radicals. He finally joined the new party by allowing his name to be placed in nomination as a delegate to an antislavery convention that was scheduled to meet in Bloomington, Illinois, on the 29th of May, 1856. In Bloomington, he was soon in the thick of debate over the Republican state platform.

There remained a formidable opposition. The Democratic Party, although wounded by sectional strife and increasingly at odds with itself over the extension of slavery, retained the loyalty of millions. Like the Republican Party, it was composed of factions that had joined together in a mutually beneficial association; its objectives were generally to oppose industrialization and modernization, to further states' rights and territorial expansion. Unlike its rival, it was truly national in character, drawing strength from every section of the Union. Despite defections, the Democrats in 1856 succeeded in papering over their disputes and presenting a unified front.

At the national convention that year, the party turned away from lackluster Franklin Pierce, rejected controversial Stephen Douglas and selected Pennsylvanian James Buchanan. This "doughface" (a Northerner with Southern sympathies) was acceptable to both the North and the South and had a unique advantage over his party rivals: He

Presidential candidate Millard Fillmore gained the endorsement of the proslavery wing of the Know-Nothings (*banner below*) in the 1856 campaign, but his loyalty to Know-Nothing tenets was suspect. During his single year of membership in the nativist, anti-Catholic organization, he attended none of its secret meetings. Furthermore, his daughter was educated by nuns.

alone had made no enemies during the debate over Kansas, for he had been off in England serving as U.S. minister. To make their ticket even more attractive, the Democrats chose John C. Breckinridge of the key state of Kentucky as their candidate for vice president. Southern yet not too Southern, Breck-

John C. Frémont, the Republican presidential candidate in 1856, had to carry Pennsylvania to win the election against Pennsylvania Democrat James Buchanan. Frémont wanted as his running mate a moderate from the Keystone State, Senator Simon Cameron, but the Republican convention saddled him with William L. Dayton of New Jersey, who failed to carry even his own state.

inridge had a sizable following in all sections of the Union.

When the Republicans journeyed to Philadelphia for their own national convention in mid-June, they realized that they were not likely to win the election against the strong Buchanan-Breckinridge ticket. Their acknowledged leader was Senator William H. Seward of New York, who was backed by a most able political manipulator named Thurlow Weed. Seward, ambitious for the presidency, conceded that 1860 would probably be a more propitious year and put up little resistance when the party leaders decided on a figurehead candidate. He was a national hero but a political newcomer—John C. Frémont, called "The Pathfinder" for his Western explorations.

There was a third candidate in the race, former President Millard Fillmore, nominated by the Southern faction of the Know-Nothings and supported by the remnants of Southern Whiggery and some conservative Whigs in the North as well. Though Fillmore had no chance of winning an electoral majority, he could hope to garner votes in the border states and possibly throw the election into the House of Representatives, where he might win as a compromise candidate.

In the North, the Republicans showed astounding strength. Thousands marched in torchlight parades shouting, "Free speech, free press, free soil, free men, Frémont and victory." Republican speakers flayed the Democrats as lackeys of the "slavocracy" and accomplices in the rape of Kansas. The Democrats answered with smear campaigns against Frémont, who was, they charged without a shred of evidence, a secret Catholic and a hypocrite who once owned slaves himself. A far more effective argument against the Republican cause was voiced by Senator Robert Toombs of Georgia, who maintained that the party's close association with abolitionism made it totally unacceptable to the South. He declared, "The election of Frémont would be the end of the Union, and ought to be."

The threat of secession had its effect. Fearing economic chaos should Frémont win, bankers and financiers in New York opened their purses to the Democrats. One financier, August Belmont, contributed the then-fantastic sum of $50,000. Editor Horace Greeley admitted that "we Frémonters have not one dollar, where the Fillmoreans and Buchanans have 10 each."

When the electoral ballots were counted, Buchanan had won by 174 votes to Frémont's 114. Though 11 Northern states had gone Republican and the combined popular vote for Frémont and Fillmore exceeded Buchanan's by 10 per cent, the Democrats had been granted a final opportunity to solve the slavery issue. Should Buchanan and his party fail, the Republicans would surely be ready to assume power and impose their own solution. A prophetic poet put it succinctly: "If months have well-nigh won the field / What may not four years do?"

The whole nation seemed to heave a great sigh of relief after the election. For the moment, Kansas was pacified and talk of disunion was muted. But the partisans were not to be distracted for long. In December, outgoing President Pierce delivered a diatribe against the Republicans, sparking anew the bitter debate between the two parties and the two sections, and incoming President Buchanan added fuel to the fire in his inaugural address on March 4, 1857. Although he had been given advance word of the Supreme

Court's Dred Scott decision, Buchanan pretended ignorance. In a devious effort to conciliate the North, he declared in his address that the future of slavery in the territories rested with their populations. Two days later the Court issued its decision and, as Buchanan had known full well, thereby undercut popular sovereignty as a meaningful ideal, at least if the Court's interpretation of the Constitution was enforced.

The South responded to the Dred Scott

Democrat James Buchanan, "Old Buck," won the presidency in 1856 with a shrewd and subtle campaign that used partisan newspapers to full advantage. Scores of small-town editors were recruited to promote him as "the people's choice" even before he announced his candidacy, and Buchanan emerged as a formidable contender seemingly without the aid of politicians.

In this Republican lampoon of the Buchanan-Breckinridge platform, a slave chained hand and foot sits astride a ram, a symbol of the Missouri Border Ruffians' violent defense of slavery in Kansas. The Democrats' sympathetic attitude toward the extension of slavery won Buchanan 14 of the 15 slave states in the 1856 presidential election.

decision with jubilation, the North with fury. More Democrats, more Whigs and more Know-Nothings prepared to cast their lot with the Republicans as that party gathered strength to contest the midterm Congressional elections of 1858. Nowhere would the issue be more dramatically fought out than in Illinois, where Abraham Lincoln, seeking a national platform, challenged the "Little Giant," Stephen Douglas, for his seat in the Senate.

United States senators were still elected, in those days, by state legislatures, with the party in control of the legislature making the selection. Public nomination of a candidate was unknown. In Illinois in 1858, the Republicans broke the mold.

Meeting in their state convention on the 16th of June, 1858, the Republicans of Illinois declared that "Abraham Lincoln is the first and only choice of Illinois for the United States Senate." In accepting the nomination, Lincoln delivered what would become one of his most famous addresses. " 'A house divided against itself cannot stand,' " he told the assembled party delegates. "I believe this government cannot endure, permanently half slave and half free. I do not expect the Union to be dissolved—I do not expect the house to fall—but I do expect it will cease to be divided. It will become all one thing or all the other."

Lincoln went on to imply a conspiracy, with Douglas a prime mover, to promote the extension of slavery, and warned that the next logical move of the Supreme Court would be to declare slavery legal not just in the territories but in the Northern states as well. Lincoln's intention was to cut the middle ground from under Douglas. He would try to hang the albatross of slavery around his opponent's neck; this would weaken the benefit Douglas derived from his break with the Buchanan administration and his repudiation of the proslavery Lecompton Constitution in Kansas.

The campaign following Lincoln's nomination lacked nothing in the way of drama. Douglas, recognizing his opponent's oratorical talents, ran hard from the beginning. "I shall have my hands full," he said of Lincoln. "He is the strong man of his party—full of wit, facts, dates—and he is the best stump speaker in the West. He is as honest as he is shrewd, and if I beat him my victory will be hardly won." In July, Douglas embarked on a speaking tour of the state. Everywhere, he was accompanied by partisans who waved banners, carried torches and played martial music to announce the arrival of the Little Giant. Hard on his heels came

Abraham Lincoln. If Douglas spoke in front of a small-town courthouse one night, Lincoln would appear there the next day to attack his opponent, employing irony and logic with equal effect.

Lincoln was accused of following Douglas because he could not get a crowd otherwise. In response, he asked for face-to-face debates. Douglas hesitated—quite reasonably, from his viewpoint. Why enhance the candidacy of a lesser-known politician by sharing a platform with him? Besides, it might be dangerous to let audiences compare Lincoln with him as a speaker. But in the end, Douglas' pugnacity got the better of him, and he agreed to a series of seven debates.

The two rivals met in seven prominent country towns in as many Congressional districts: Alton, Charleston, Galesburg, Ottawa, Freeport, Jonesboro, Quincy. Yet so great was their pulling power and so momentous were the issues they discussed, that many people—and of course the press—came from far and wide to hear their arguments. To a degree unprecedented in a statewide canvass, the entire country was caught up in this contest.

In speech after speech, Douglas never weakened in defense of his favorite doctrine, popular sovereignty. Yet he aired more than political theory. Believing that blacks were inherently inferior to whites, Douglas declared that Lincoln's views would inevitably lead to granting blacks full political and social equality. He played frankly upon the prejudices of the voters. Knowing that many whites were opposed to slavery and biased against blacks, he appealed to racists by stating that the government "was established upon the white basis. It was made by white men, for the benefit of white men."

Douglas did not feel that the Negroes should necessarily be slaves, but in his opinion they should not necessarily be free either. That was a decision for whites. He declared that moral arguments had no place in the discussion and that he was fighting for the great principle of self-government. To his opponent's assertion that the nation could not endure half slave and half free, Douglas rejoined that diversity in local and domestic institutions was "the great safeguard of our liberties." These representations confirmed Lincoln's earlier opinion that Douglas seemed to have "no very vivid impression that the Negro is human."

A similar charge might well have been leveled at Lincoln. Stung by Douglas' attacks that his program would bring black equality, Lincoln associated himself with views that were both antislavery and antiblack—at least when he spoke in southern Illinois, where Democratic sentiment was strong. In Charleston, for example, Lincoln remarked: "I am not . . . in favor of bringing about . . . the social and political equality of the white and black races—I am not . . . in favor of making voters or jurors of Negroes, nor of qualifying them to hold office, nor to intermarry with white people. And inasmuch as they [blacks and whites] cannot so live, while they do remain together there must be the position of superior and inferior, and I as much as any other man am in favor of having the superior position assigned to the white race." At other times, and when addressing more liberal audiences, Lincoln would take a high-minded tack. In one speech he urged his audience to stop arguing about race and unite as one people, "declaring that all men are created equal."

Over all, the contest was about even, but

Wearing a stovepipe hat, Stephen Douglas campaigns from an open carriage *(center)* in Chicago on the 9th of July, 1858. That night, a dramatic fireworks display, cannonades and rocket barrages set the stage for the Little Giant's opening speech in the Senatorial race against Lincoln.

at Freeport, Douglas committed a tactical error. Replying to the charge that the Dred Scott decision had jeopardized popular sovereignty, denying territorial voters the right to decide whether to enter the Union as a free state or as a slave state, Douglas suggested that the Court's ruling was itself a nullity. Slavery, he insisted, could only exist in those territories where a majority of the people desired it and protected it with police power. In territories where there was no liking for slavery, it could not survive, because the populace would deny it protection. "Hence, no matter what the decision of the Supreme Court," he stated, "the right of the people to make a slave Territory or a free Territory is perfect and complete." In the South, where Douglas' defection on the Lecompton Constitution had already cost him wide support, he was anathematized for this Freeport Doctrine, which suggested that the proslavery Dred Scott decision could be ignored with impunity.

When the voters of Illinois finally went to the polls, the Republicans outvoted the pro-Douglas Democrats by a margin of 125,000 to 121,000. However, the legislative districts had been realigned, which gave Douglas a majority in the state house and one more term in the Senate.

Lincoln, in defeat, had gained more than he lost: The debates with Douglas had elevated him to national stature. With 1860 a mere two years distant, men like Horace Greeley could now look to Lincoln as a compromise presidential candidate. The path to the White House that led through the great auditorium at Cooper Union had begun in the tiny Illinois townships where Lincoln found his platform.

Naturally enough, Lincoln was dejected

THE CAMPAIGN IN ILLINOIS.

THE LAST JOINT DEBATE.

DOUGLAS AND LINCOLN AT ALTON.

5,000 TO 10,000 PERSONS PRESENT!

LINCOLN AGAIN REFUSES TO ANSWER WHETHER HE WILL VOTE TO ADMIT KANSAS IF HER PEOPLE APPLY WITH A CONSTITUTION RECOGNIZING SLAVERY.

APPEARS IN HIS OLD CHARACTER OF THE "ARTFUL DODGER."

TRIES TO PALM HIMSELF OFF TO THE WHIGS OF MADISON COUNTY AS A FRIEND OF HENRY CLAY AND NO ABOLITIONIST, AND IS EXPOSED!!

GREAT SPEECHES OF SENATOR DOUGLAS.

by his defeat. As the election returns drifted in and Douglas' victory became obvious, Lincoln left his law office to walk home. It was dark, the path was worn slick, and he lost his footing. He caught himself on his hands just before he hit the ground, then got up and walked on home. Years later, he remembered saying to himself, "It's a slip and not a fall."

No sooner had Congress convened in December 1859 than the sectional controversy found a new focus: the Speakership of the House of Representatives, where the Republicans held a plurality but not a majority. Their candidate for Speaker was John Sherman of Ohio, and normally, as the leading party's choice, his election would have been assured. But not this time. The Republicans had only a 10-vote plurality, and Sherman made his election difficult by endorsing a digest of a book entitled *The Impending Crisis of*

An article in the frankly partisan *Chicago Daily Times* portrays Lincoln as a slippery character who behaved in an "improper and ungentlemanly" fashion in his debate with Douglas in Alton, Illinois.

routine manner. True or not, the protest did nothing to soothe his opponents.

Behind the arguments that raged over the Speakership lay an increasing sense of Southern impotence. As the Republicans gained strength in Washington, Southern members of the House fell back on tactics of deadlock and delay. Tempers went wild as the debate heated up. "The only persons who do not have a revolver and knife," bemoaned Senator James H. Hammond from across the rotunda, "are those who have two revolvers." On the floor of the House, O. R. Singleton of Mississippi called for disunion and war, while Illinois Representative John A. Logan waved a pistol and shouted at the gallery, "By God, if I can't talk, I can do something else!" Eventually Sherman withdrew, and on the 44th ballot a compromise candidate, Republican William Pennington of New Jersey, was selected.

Throughout the contest for the Speakership, the Southern Representatives had been much less concerned about Sherman's views than about the Northern attitude toward the death of John Brown. On December 2, 1859, when the old fanatic had gone to the gallows, church bells in Northern towns tolled a mournful tribute. To many Southerners, this was an endorsement of the atrocity and meant that they had better prepare to fight.

So a new decade began with the issue truly joined—Union or disunion, war or peace. One hope remained, albeit a forlorn hope, and that lay with the Democrats in the upcoming presidential election. If the Democrats could settle on a candidate who appealed to all factions, they might well defeat the Republicans. If the party chose a candidate who alienated any significant segment of the party, it was abundantly clear that a

the South. The author, a 27-year-old poor white named Hinton Helper, attacked slavery not out of sympathy for the slaves but because he believed that the institution was creating a permanent class of impoverished whites. In any case, wealthy and influential Southerners feared that the Helper tract would foment rebellion among the region's lower classes.

Congressman John B. Clark of Missouri introduced a resolution saying that no member of the House who endorsed the Helper doctrine was fit to be Speaker. Though the resolution never passed, it started a battle royal. Realizing that he had caused more trouble than he could handle, Sherman declared that he had not even read the offending volume and had endorsed it in a purely

Republican, perhaps an out-and-out abolitionist, would be elected President, with civil war a likelihood.

Everything went wrong for the Democrats from the first. In an ill-advised selection of convention site, intended to reassure the South, the Democrats decided to meet in Charleston, South Carolina, the very heart of secessionist sentiment, where the fire-eaters of Dixie would be playing to a home audience. Most Northern Democrats arrived for the opening gavel on April 23 determined to reject the Southerners' demand for a pro-slavery plank and backing a candidate repugnant to the South, Stephen Douglas. The South would have neither. Addressing the gathering, the veteran Alabama radical William L. Yancey laid down his terms before his Northern colleagues: unconditional surrender. In a blunt warning that Northern Democrats must adopt a platform calling for a federal slave code that would protect the rights of slaveholders anywhere in the Union, he declared, "We are in a position to ask you to yield." The Northerners refused, and Yancey headed a walkout of 50 Southern delegates.

When voting for the presidential nomination got under way, it soon became painfully clear that, with 50 fewer delegates on hand, neither the front-runner Douglas nor anyone else had the necessary two thirds of the full convention needed for the nomination. After 57 ballots, the delegates were so exhausted and depressed that they voted to adjourn until June 18 and then try again in a less partisan place, Baltimore. "The proceedings at Charleston," wrote John Breckinridge, "threaten great calamities, unless there is wisdom and forbearance enough to redeem errors, at Baltimore."

But wisdom and forbearance were still in short supply when the Democrats reconvened. Failing once more to get a tolerable platform, Southerners again walked out, and 110 delegates set up their own rump convention nearby. With so many opposition delegates gone and a simple majority rule instituted, Stephen Douglas had two thirds of the remaining votes; he easily won the nomination—and with it a hopeless cause.

The Southern Democrats, for their part, wanted Breckinridge to run for President. He refused to let his name be used at a seceders' convention. Despite his disavowals, Breckinridge was nominated on a platform that called for the federal government to "protect the rights of persons and property in the Territories and wherever else its Constitutional authority extended." This was a platform on which the South could stand but not win. Upon being informed of his selection, Breckinridge was appalled and decided to decline the honor.

Opposition to the Republicans was further fragmented by a faction of Whigs who had reconstituted themselves as the Constitutional Union Party and had chosen as their standard-bearer John Bell of Tennessee. Bell was expected to run not on a platform but on a platitude: "The Constitution of the Country, the Union of the States, and the enforcement of the laws."

Then came the last attempts at compromise and statesmanship that the country would see for some time. Mississippi Senator Jefferson Davis realized that the split in the Democratic Party virtually guaranteed a victory for the hated Republicans. He proposed that Breckinridge accept the nomination, for he assumed Douglas would then realize that his own candidacy was futile. At that point a deal would be struck: Douglas, Breckinridge and Bell would all withdraw in favor of some compromise nominee who could unify the various anti-Republican elements under one umbrella. Bell agreed early to the scheme, and now Breckinridge did so too. He accepted his nomination and waited for Douglas to withdraw, so that he too could make a graceful exit.

But Douglas declined his prescribed part. After years of effort he had a presidential nomination, and he was not going to give it up. His refusal wiped out Davis' compromise. Three candidates were left in the field to oppose the Republicans.

Between the two Democratic meetings in Charleston and Baltimore, the Republicans held their own convention in Chicago, where an enormous frame building called the Wigwam was hastily thrown up to accommodate them. Despite the party's seriousness of purpose, the Republicans came to Chicago in a raucous mood. The delegations were accompanied by 900 reporters and thousands of hangers-on who came in claques to flood the Wigwam and stampede the convention for one candidate or another. Lincoln's Illinois supporters were among the most numerous, since they had the shortest distance to go. And Lincoln's astute managers printed up hundreds of tickets to hand out to Honest Abe's enthusiasts, so that the followers of Lincoln's archrival, William Seward of New York, could not dominate the crowds.

The sectional nature of the Republican Party could hardly escape notice. There were few representatives from the border states, and those who did come represented constituencies of dubious size and commitment. The Deep South sent not a single representative, though a group from Michigan proclaimed itself the Texas delegation. Another example of geographic prestidigitation was supplied by Horace Greeley. An anti-Seward New Yorker, he had been barred from his home state's delegation by its pro-Seward party boss, Thurlow Weed. Politically following his own advice to "Go West, young man," Greeley wangled an appointment to the Oregon delegation.

In contrast to their contentious Democratic rivals, the Republicans were most obliging in carpentering their platform. Hoping to gain support from moderates, anti-Douglas Democrats and Whigs—and at the same time to lay to rest its radical reputation—the party adopted a mildly worded platform. A protective-tariff plank appealed to businessmen and a homestead plank expressed the yearnings of thousands of Americans for cheap land beyond the Mississippi. There was something for just about everyone in the Republican platform; even Southern slaveholders were vaguely assured the sanctity of their property rights.

The desire of the party to appear moderate had a powerful effect on its choice of presidential candidate. Seward, the front runner at first, did not come across as a moderate, though his prediction several years earlier of an "irrepressible conflict" between North and South made him appear far more radical and intransigent than he actually was. Besides, his long years in high political office had made him almost as many powerful enemies as friends. His support outside his home state and New England was shallow.

Still, other candidates had similar problems. Edward Bates of Missouri, having flirted with the Know-Nothings, had earned the enmity of the many German-Americans, and Simon Cameron of Pennsylvania suf-

111

l's Political Chart, a popular
to the 1860 presidential
on, was crammed with portraits
umbnail sketches of the
dates and platforms, as well as
onal map—all sandwiched
en two files of past presidents.

fered from a reputation as a political fixer and ideological wanderer whose travels had carried him into the Democratic, Whig and Know-Nothing Parties before he finally settled down as a Republican. Cameron could not count on the wholehearted support of even his home-state delegation.

There were other candidates with the credentials to compete for the Republican Party nomination. Among them were Salmon P. Chase of Ohio and U.S. Supreme Court Justice John McLean. There was also Lincoln, considered moderate on the slavery issue, properly conservative on the tariff and on the construction of transportation facilities, free of the Know-Nothing taint, and just prominent enough to have made his mark without acquiring too many enemies. As Lincoln himself realized, few delegates aside from his Illinois friends were committed to his candidacy, but he had become the second choice of many and would be in a good position should front-runner Seward falter. Just before the convention opened, he wrote to a friend: "My name is new in the field; and I suppose I am not the first choice of a very great many. Our policy, then, is to give no offence to others—leave them in a mood to come to us, if they shall be impelled to give up their first love."

From the beginning, Lincoln's managers took to the floor, buttonholing delegates, cajoling waverers, promising jobs great and small in the Lincoln administration. Back home in Springfield, where he was awaiting the vote, Lincoln dispatched a telegram to his supporters: "I authorize no bargains and will be bound by none." Whether Lincoln really hoped to disavow deals or merely wished to show clean hands, he well knew that patronage was the grease of politics, and

David Davis, his convention manager, paid no heed to his message except to remark perfunctorily, "Lincoln ain't here and don't know what we have to meet, so we will go ahead as if we hadn't heard from him, and he must ratify it."

Davis' deals paid off. On the first ballot Seward led, as expected, but drew only 173½ votes, while Lincoln was stronger than expected with 102. On the second ballot, Cameron and Bates began to falter. Lincoln's tally increased to 181 while Seward inched forward to just 184½, an ominous sign for the New Yorker. The third ballot confirmed the trend: Seward dropped back to 180 and Lincoln surged to 231½, just a vote and a half short of the nomination. Before that roll call ended, a delegate from Ohio leaped to his feet and shouted: "I arise, Mr. Chairman, to announce the change of four votes of Ohio from Mr. Chase to Mr. Lincoln."

Abraham Lincoln was over the top, and the convention broke into a roar of approbation. Outside the Wigwam someone fired a cannon, and boat whistles shrieked on Lake Michigan.

Thus there would be four candidates of as many political outlooks. Breckinridge represented protection of slavery in the territories; Douglas held fast to popular sovereignty; Lincoln stood for containing slavery in the states where it then existed and looked forward to a time when the practice would perish, presumably of natural causes; and Bell studiously wished away the present strife and looked backward to a time when the slave question hardly ruffled the surface of domestic tranquillity.

In the campaign that followed, the complex slave issue became secondary to the threat of disunion. Breckinridge, supported

113

In full regalia, the Wide-Awake sported a hat and a cape and carried a rail (a reference to Lincoln the Railsplitter) topped by a tin lamp for nocturnal marches. The group's name came from the hat members wore: Made of a fabric that had no nap, it was punningly referred to as a wide-awake.

The Wide-Awakes: Lighting a Path for "Old Abe"

"Broadway was one river of fire, as though Vesuvius had poured forth a torrent of molten lava." The reporter who wrote those lines was describing one of the many torchlight parades of the Wide-Awakes—in this case, through New York City on the night of October 3, 1860. Wide-Awakes were young Republicans, zealous and downright tireless in their campaigning to get Abraham Lincoln elected President.

The phenomenon began in Hartford, Connecticut, in March of 1860, when about 50 young men formed a club and adopted bizarre uniforms. Amid the overheated politics of the time, the idea proved contagious: Wide-Awake groups sprang up everywhere; East Chatham, New York, even had a club of daring young women. When Lincoln rode to victory on Election Day, November 6, his loudest boosters were no fewer than 400,000 Wide-Awakes.

A group of Wide-Awakes from Mohawk, New York, assembles for a demonstration. Their marching song was "Ain't You Glad You Joined the Republicans?"

by avowed secessionists though deeply attached to the Union, found himself on the defensive in the North and the border regions. Lincoln was attacked not as a disunionist but as one whose election would assuredly bring about that result. For his part, Douglas saw himself as the realistic compromise, the only candidate with support in every section, the one man who could cool passions and bring a new unity to the nation. Recognizing that the odds favored Lincoln, he alone among the four broke with tradition and personally took to the hustings. Wherever he could gain a platform, whether in Massachusetts, Illinois or North Carolina, the stocky little Senator deplored with equal vigor the secessionists of the South and the abolitionists of the North.

The campaign was tumultuous throughout the North, South and West. In every town, partisans held parades, threw picnics and bellowed speeches. Liberty and Union were the watchwords of Republican orators in abolitionist New England; Union and economic growth were their themes in the Middle Atlantic States, where slavery was less compelling. In the South, the local press, bracing for the anticipated victory of Lincoln, sounded the secessionist battle cry. An Atlanta journal went so far as to say, "We regard every man an enemy to the institutions of the South who does not boldly declare that he believes African slavery to be a social, moral and political blessing." The Charleston *Mercury* was particularly vitriolic, branding Lincoln "the beau ideal of a relentless, dogged, free-soil Border Ruffian, a vulgar mobocrat and a Southern hater." And rather than "submit to such humiliation and degradation as the inauguration of Abraham Lincoln," proclaimed another South-

Abraham Lincoln was eloquently portrayed by photographers, but his quick-changing facial expressions were beyond the reach of the camera of the day. When Lincoln spoke, recalled a *Chicago Tribune* editor, "the dull, listless features dropped like a mask. The whole countenance was wreathed in animation."

"Honest Abe" Lincoln gallops toward the White House as a quartet of jubilant blacks carry off the body of John C. Breckinridge, the Southern Democrats' candidate for President. Though such campaign symbolism succeeded in the North, it backfired in the South, where Lincoln was looked upon as a rabid abolitionist and archenemy of whites

Greeting local Republicans, Abraham Lincoln towers above supporters at the front door of his house in Springfield, Illinois, during a rally in August of 1860.

ern newspaper, the South would see "the Potomac crimsoned in human gore, and Pennsylvania Avenue paved ten fathoms deep with mangled bodies."

Northern and Republican newspapers answered in kind, but for the most part refused to take Southern talk of secession seriously. They declared the threats of disunion to be "the idlest gossip imaginable," intended "to bully the people out of their choice," and with blind optimism they announced that Lincoln's election, far from bringing disunion, would inaugurate "a time of actual repose and peace quite unheard of for the last 10 years."

Lincoln himself looked upon the secession talk as essentially bluff and bluster. He pointed to the fact that all the candidates, even Breckinridge, opposed secession, and he placed his faith in the South's underlying attachment to the Union. When asked to issue a statement reassuring the South that slavery would be protected in those states where it existed, Lincoln refused, stating that he had already made his stand on that point abundantly clear.

The first significant portents of a Republican victory came in October, when state elections were held in Pennsylvania and Indiana, where Northern Democrats thought they stood a chance. In both states, Republicans swept the field. Douglas read these signs clearly. "Mr. Lincoln is the next President," he said. "We must try to save the Union. I will go South." Submerging his personal ambition, disregarding his failing health, Douglas plunged into Dixie, imploring and demanding that, whatever the outcome in November, the Union be preserved. But the South had read the same portents and agreed that all of them pointed to disunion. Many

baseless rumors stiffened Southern resolve. Abolitionists, it was said, had invaded Texas and were poisoning wells. Tales of slave rebellions, reported as fact in the press, added fear to the impulses galvanizing the South. The few Southern voices of moderation went unheeded. During his tour of Dixie, Douglas occasionally met with courtesy, occasionally met with boos, but always his save-the-Union preachments were wasted on the soft Southern air.

Election Day (the 6th of November, 1860) found Douglas on the road in Mobile, Alabama, and Lincoln at home in Springfield. At nightfall in Illinois, the telegraph reported that the state had gone Republican. Indiana soon followed suit. Then came a flood of Republican returns from the other states of the Northwest. Before midnight, Pennsylvania—home state of President Buchanan—fell into the Republican column. When heavily Republican returns began to flow in from New York, the state with the largest electoral vote in the nation, the election of Lincoln was certain.

The citizens of Springfield went wild. The President-elect walked over to a reception where refreshments were available. He was serenaded by the crowd. Among his well-wishers were people who had undoubtedly voted for Douglas; Lincoln had failed to carry his home county.

When the final returns were at last recorded, the electoral vote reflected with appalling accuracy the sectional split within the country. Lincoln had carried every free state except New Jersey, which divided its electors between the two Illinois candidates. South of the Mason-Dixon line, Lincoln carried nothing—indeed, many Southern states had not even placed his name on the ballot. Bell, the

Anti-Lincoln headlines, vowing to form a Southern nation, lure readers to a mundane clothing advertisement published in the Charleston *Courier*. In fact, the South Carolinians were so rebellious that a local college president wrote: "You might as well attempt to control a tornado as to attempt to stop them from secession."

Constitutional Union candidate, captured Virginia, Kentucky and Tennessee. The rest of the South went solidly for Breckinridge. Douglas ended up with three of New Jersey's seven votes and all of Missouri's nine. Lincoln, with 180 electoral votes, had won a majority and was the next President.

The popular vote, however, told a more equivocal story. The combined opposition outpolled Lincoln by almost a million votes. Even in the free states, Lincoln's total majority was under 300,000; he would assume office with only a tenuous hold on the people of his own region. Arrayed against him were the seven states of the Deep South and undoubtedly, once they had time to adjust to realities, the four states of the Upper South. However the border states had voted, no one could foretell which side they would take in case of Southern secession.

In spite of the terrific momentum toward secession, a final effort was made to reconcile the South and salvage the Union. A committee of 13 Senators, led by John J. Crittenden of Kentucky, put forth a proposal to reestablish the Missouri Compromise line and extend it to California, permitting slavery in the territories south of latitude 36° 30′. The committee members also attempted to strengthen the Fugitive Slave Law and to make their amendments unrepealable and unamendable for all time.

Crittenden hoped to have the plan adopted by Congress and then put to a referendum. If he had succeeded, there is little doubt that the referendum would have been approved. But the Republicans were opposed, so the proposal was killed on the Senate floor. Crittenden would have a special reason for regretting the failure of his compromise: His sons Thomas and George would serve as generals on opposite sides in the fratricidal conflict ahead.

Yet even after the Crittenden Compromise failed, it did not quite die. It was resurrected in the form of seven Constitutional amendments and presented in Washington in a last-ditch peace assemblage that some observers called the "old men's convention." Elderly, shopworn politicians—the likes of former President John Tyler and David Wilmot, the author of the Wilmot Proviso—droned on for days. The Senate rejected their proposals and the House refused to consider the results of the convention, and that, at last, was the end of it.

Meanwhile, the South was reacting vigorously to the election of its bête noire, Lincoln. The agitators for secession were in control; their years of whipping up Southern passions and Southern patriotism had borne fruit at last. The aged provocator Edmund Ruffin had actually prayed for Lincoln's election because he hoped that South Carolina would secede from the Union, and that other states would do the same. Ruffin traveled to Charleston to watch his hope turn to prophecy. The breakup of the Union began on December 20, when delegates from all over South Carolina met in Charleston and voted unanimously to pull the state out of the Union. Charleston rejoiced. Mary Boykin Chesnut, the vivacious wife of a South Carolina aristocrat who owned several plantations and as many as 500 slaves, wrote in her diary, "We are divorced, North and South, because we have hated each other so."

Charleston had become a tinderbox, needing only one spark to explode into war—one spark in a city full of firebrands.

Storm over Sumter

*"Why did that green goose Anderson go into Fort Sumter?
Then everything began to go wrong."*

MARY BOYKIN CHESNUT

The man who decided where the Civil War would begin arrived in Charleston in late November of 1860, about two weeks after Lincoln's election and four weeks before the secession of South Carolina. He was Major Robert Anderson, the new commander of the three Federal forts in Charleston Harbor: Moultrie, Sumter and Castle Pinckney.

Anderson had been appointed to his post by President Buchanan's subversive Secretary of War, John B. Floyd, because he came from good Kentucky stock, was married to a Georgia woman, had owned slaves and would presumably act with Southern bias in the looming crisis. Floyd, whose loyalty was to his native Virginia, was busily sending guns south to Federal installations where secessionist militia units could easily supply themselves when hostilities broke out.

Anderson's appointment suited another Virginian, General in Chief of the United States Army Winfield Scott, for the opposite reason. Scott, the greatest and, at 74, oldest American military hero, never wavered in his loyalty to the national government, and he was convinced that Anderson would not waver either. Anderson had served as Scott's aide during the Mexican War, and though he had shown no signs of outstanding talent, his determination and devotion to duty had driven him so hard that it took three bullets to knock him out of action.

Anderson viewed his Charleston assignment with healthy trepidation. He realized that his slightest misstep or miscalculation could touch off general warfare—a chilling responsibility. Besides, he was haunted by the past. By an odd coincidence, his father, Captain Richard Anderson, had defended Fort Moultrie in Charleston Harbor during the American Revolution, and had been forced to surrender to the British. The major feared he might repeat family history.

Above all, Anderson worried about his defensive posture. His main base, Fort Moultrie, on big Sullivan's Island, commanding the northern entrance to Charleston Harbor *(map, page 150)*, was terribly vulnerable to land attack from the rear; in fact, Moultrie, with its 1,500 feet of works, was much too much fort to be held by Anderson's meager force of 60 Regular Army soldiers.

Castle Pinckney, lying less than a mile off the coast of Charleston, was unmanned and poorly armed, but it could be an effective counterthreat if only Anderson had enough troops and guns to garrison it properly; cannon in position here could do so much damage to the city that Confederate troublemakers might leave Moultrie alone.

But if worst came to worst, the most advantageous place for Anderson to make a stand was clearly Fort Sumter, on a tiny island 3.3 miles from Charleston. Although hasty efforts to strengthen this installation were still incomplete, Anderson's predecessor had laid in enough supplies to last for several months, and Sumter's guns could answer any attack by closing the harbor to Southern shipping to and from the city.

Anderson fully expected South Carolina to secede and to attack his fort. So he quickly began pelting the War Department in Washington with urgent reports of his shortages and requests for firm orders. Was he to surrender his forts if and when South Carolina so demanded? If not, when could he count on reinforcements? He must have troops to garrison Castle Pinckney, and to man the guns at Fort Sumter, where only an engineer and some workmen were stationed. As for Fort Moultrie, he told Secretary of War Floyd that South Carolina's intention "to obtain possession of this work, is apparent to all," and that Floyd must help him thwart that design at once. "The clouds are threatening," Anderson warned, "and the storm may break at any moment."

Floyd did nothing to help. He even declined to mention Anderson's appeals to General Scott, who could have offered his former colleague sound advice. On December 1 the Secretary informed Anderson that no reinforcements would be sent, since there would be no attack on the forts. But he finally gave Anderson a little maneuvering room.

On orders from Floyd, Major Don Carlos Buell traveled to Charleston on December 9 and spent two days inspecting the forts. In private discussion with Anderson, Buell relayed Floyd's permission for the major to defend any fort of his choice if attacked. Anderson could also move his command to the most defensible fort if he acquired evidence of hostile plans by the South Carolinians.

Evidence of hostility abounded. As early as November 12, South Carolina authorities had stationed 20 militiamen to "protect" the Federal arsenal in Charleston—that is, to deny its arms and munitions to the rightful owners. And more evidence poured in. On December 20, South Carolina seceded as expected. Henceforth, bands of armed secessionists from Moultrieville, a small town outside Moultrie's walls, patrolled the boundary of the fort day and night, and the Federal officers there were soon so exhausted by their tense hours on duty that two of them let their wives take their shift. Casual exchanges between soldiers and local people were virtually cut off. Militia companies from all over South Carolina kept pouring into Charleston, and rumors of Rebel attack plans grew ever more numerous and intimidating.

For a while, Anderson felt that his duty was crystal clear. He was to avoid a clash if honor permitted; if not, he would defend his Federal enclave by strength of arms. But then on December 23 he received a note from Secretary Floyd that threw him into uncertainty again. The message seemed to suggest that if he was attacked, he should surrender rather than suffer pointless casualties. Suspecting Floyd's political motives and feeling abandoned by Washington, the major decided that the time had come to act. He would shift all his men to Fort Sumter on Christmas night and brace to face any emergency.

Anderson kept his plans quiet. On his unexplained orders, his soldiers and civilian workers spent all Christmas Day packing Moultrie's movable goods. Rain postponed the transfer that night. But the next night the men ferried their gear to Sumter so furtively that the crowds in Charleston suspected nothing until the following day, the 27th.

That morning they saw—across the water at Moultrie—smoke rising from the wooden gun carriages that the Federals had set afire to deny the secessionists use of the cannon. But it was not until noon that the Charlestonians and all the secessionists, gazing toward

The dapper young officers of a Charleston militia company assembl with their men at nearby Castle Pinckney, an undefended Federal for they took over on December 27, 1860. The South Carolinians had found a single Union officer supervising workmen in the fort, and they courteously permitted him to join his command on Fort Sumter.

Sumter, realized that the fort was now fully garrisoned: The Stars and Stripes was being raised on the mast atop the ramparts. The secessionists reacted quickly, seizing Moultrie, the Federal arsenal in Charleston, the post office and the customs house.

Naturally, Anderson's move to Sumter was damned throughout the South as aggression. Naturally, too, Northerners praised the major for defying the disloyal Southerners. Anderson received a fair amount of fan mail, which the secessionists dutifully delivered. One admirer wrote: "The Lord bless your noble soul! Oh, my dear sir, the whole country will triumphantly sustain you."

Of course, Anderson had not intended his move to be aggressive or defiant. On the contrary, he hoped that by occupying a stronger position he would prevent or at least delay an outbreak of hostilities. Perhaps he did manage to postpone the war.

But with passing time, Sumter swelled in symbolic importance to the North and South, becoming an issue in itself. The fort was a Federal installation from which the United States could not retreat, and it was also a piece of South Carolina property that that self-declared sovereign state refused to leave in the hands of a so-called foreign power. Unwittingly, Anderson had made Fort Sumter the final cause and first objective of the unavoidable war.

The conflicting orders that so dismayed Anderson were a natural product of the utter confusion that reigned in Washington. The trouble began at the top. President Buchanan, always a weak executive, was now a lame duck to boot. Ill-informed and largely ignored, depressed by events beyond his control, believing it was Congress' responsibility to act, he vacillated, hoping that critical decisions could be deferred until he left office in March 1861. Buchanan apparently did not learn of Anderson's move to Fort Sumter until the day after the event, and then he was told not by his staff but by three Southern callers, among them Senator Jefferson Davis. "My God," the President groaned, "are calamities never to come singly?"

Another misfortune arrived at the White House on December 28 in the form of three commissioners from the state of South Carolina, appointed by the secession convention to negotiate with Buchanan for Anderson's removal, or for possession of Fort Sumter by purchase if need be. The President received them, which amounted to diplomatic recognition of South Carolina. Then he put off a decision until he could consult with his Cabinet. And he consulted as long as possible.

The Cabinet was now in the throes of therapeutic change. Floyd was under a dark cloud for financial corruption as well as for his political disloyalty, and so was Secretary of the Interior Jacob Thompson of Louisiana. Indeed, the cloud over Floyd was so black that Buchanan had already asked for his resignation—not face to face, at the risk of unpleasantries, but by sending Vice President Breckinridge. Floyd had agreed to resign but declined to hurry, and Buchanan did nothing to force the issue. But, in any case, the Southerners who had dominated the Cabinet were on their way out.

When the Cabinet met, Floyd undid himself completely by claiming that Anderson had disobeyed his orders in moving to Sumter. That allegation was proved false when someone produced a memorandum of the instructions Floyd had given Major Buell to deliver verbally to Anderson. Now, the Union men in the Cabinet—Attorney General Edwin M. Stanton, Postmaster General Joseph Holt and the newly appointed Secretary of State Jeremiah Black—gained the

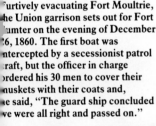

Furtively evacuating Fort Moultrie, the Union garrison sets out for Fort Sumter on the evening of December 26, 1860. The first boat was intercepted by a secessionist patrol craft, but the officer in charge ordered his 30 men to cover their muskets with their coats and, he said, "The guard ship concluded we were all right and passed on."

Kneeling in newly occupied Fort Sumter, Union Major Robert Anderson (*left*) joins his men in a prayer of thanksgiving for their safe passage from Fort Moultrie. The Stars and Stripes was then raised, the band played "Hail Columbia" and the troops presented arms.

upper hand. Though this meeting and the next failed to wring a decision from the President, his resistance to his former Southern friends was itself a victory for the Union men. And the next day Buchanan continued to put off the Carolina commissioners: "You don't give me time to consider," he complained, "you don't give me time to say my prayers. I always say my prayers when required to act upon any great State affair."

It took several more Cabinet meetings before Buchanan made up his mind. In the midst of it all, Floyd finally resigned and Thompson prepared to do so. When the President's answer came, it was no. Anderson would not be ordered to leave Sumter. On December 30, Buchanan gave that word to the South Carolina commissioners and, more remarkable still, added that Sumter would be defended "against hostile attacks from whatever quarter they may come."

At last Buchanan was trying to get a grip on events. And the effort turned up some distressing news. After listening to blunt talk concerning the political situation from Robert Toombs, another once-influential Southerner, the President exclaimed, "Good God, Mr. Toombs, do you mean that I am in the midst of a revolution?"

"Yes, sir," Toombs replied. "More than that, you have been there for a year and have not yet found it out."

Unfortunately for Buchanan, his decision to offend South Carolina and keep Fort Sumter gave rise to a new problem: the need, called to his attention in a letter from General Scott, for an expedition to bolster Sumter with men and supplies. Buchanan had no choice but to agree, and thereby almost started the war three months early.

Buchanan left the enterprise in Scott's

usually capable hands. The general ordered four companies of Regulars at Fort Monroe in Virginia to prepare for embarkation on the U.S.S. *Brooklyn* and to take three months' supplies. But then Scott fell into Buchanan's habit of temporizing. He thought it only courteous to wait until the commissioners could study the President's reply. He worried that the deep-draft warship might run aground on the shoals outside Charleston Harbor. Further, he abandoned his own idea of using troops from Fort Monroe: It was unwise to weaken that garrison, for Virginia might at any time secede as well. No doubt it would be safer to use troops from New York.

After all of his cogitation, Scott decided against a simple, overt relief expedition and ordered a tricky, clandestine operation. He had his Assistant Adjutant General Lorenzo Thomas engage a merchant vessel, the *Star of the West*, at the exorbitant sum of $1,250 per day. The idea was that the *Star*, which regularly traveled between New York and New Orleans, could depart unnoticed with a secret cargo of 200 troops. Thomas made all arrangements privately so that no intelligence of his doings would go through normal government channels. The soldiers chosen for the expedition were told to stay below-decks as they approached Charleston Harbor, so that the South Carolinians would see only the ship's crew and would assume that another plain merchantman was arriving.

Well after dark on January 5, 1861, the *Star of the West* quietly left her berth in New York and started on her way. For all the earnest attempts at secrecy, word of the expedition quickly became public knowledge. Two days after the ship sailed, rumors of her mission began to appear in the New York press, and in Washington both Interior Secretary Thompson and Senator Louis T. Wigfall of Texas learned more than enough about the plan. Thompson on January 8 notified South Carolina of the relief expedition and then, at last, resigned his Cabinet post. At the same time, Wigfall telegraphed to Governor Francis Pickens of South Carolina that the ship could be expected in Charleston Harbor at any hour. Unlike Thompson, who hurried home to Mississippi, Wigfall remained in Washington for two months, ferreting out news to send south.

While the *Star* was en route, Joseph Holt, who had shifted from postmaster general to replace Floyd as Secretary of War, was alarmed by a delayed dispatch from Anderson. The major said that he now felt quite secure, that he did not need reinforcement for the moment, and that the secessionists were building gun emplacements along the shore commanding the main ship channel to Sumter. At once Holt concluded that the *Star* was risking destruction, and possibly war, for no worthwhile purpose. He tried to call the ship back, but it was too late.

The worst of it was that Anderson did not know a relief ship was coming his way. Holt had sent him detailed information of the plan, along with permission to open fire should the *Star* be shelled. But the letter, on which war might hinge, was sent through the regular mails instead of by courier, and it would not arrive until after the event. The only advance warning Anderson received came on January 8, when a copy of the Charleston *Mercury* was brought to the fort by a workman. It carried the news that the Union relief ship *Star of the West* was expected to arrive that night or the following morning. Lacking any official notification to that effect, Anderson dismissed the report.

OUR NATIONAL BIRD AS IT APPEARED WHEN HANDED TO JAMES BUCHANAN. MARCH 4.1857.

THE IDENTICAL BIRD AS IT APPEARED .A .D. 1861.

A slashing 1860 attack on the Democrats alleges that four years of the Buchanan administration have transformed the once-proud American eagle into a plucked bird.

commit the nation to war under circumstances he did not understand. Within minutes the *Star of the West* turned about, unable to stand the shelling. She suffered two minor hits while passing Morris Island but made her way safely back to the open sea.

It was a frustrating and humiliating experience for the Sumter garrison. Anderson angrily sent Governor Pickens a note demanding an explanation and threatening to use his guns to close the harbor unless Pickens apologized for the shelling of the *Star*. Of course the Governor declined; he said that his batteries had merely acted in defense, but if Anderson opened fire, then that would be an act of aggression. In the end, the two lapsed into something resembling a truce.

But passions in Charleston and elsewhere were too inflamed by the episode to accept a truce. Robert Barnwell Rhett, the fire-eating editor of the Charleston *Mercury*, wrote that "powder has been burnt over the decree of our State, timber has been crashed, perhaps blood spilled." The firing on the *Star of the West* was "the opening ball of the Revolution," and South Carolina was honored to be the first thus to resist the Yankee tyranny. "She has not hesitated to strike the first blow, full in the face of her insulter," Rhett exclaimed. "We would not exchange or recall that blow for millions! It has wiped out a half century of scorn and outrage."

The North entertained opinions hardly less vehement. "The authority and dignity of the Government must be vindicated at every hazard," declared the Albany, New York, *Atlas and Argus*. "The issue thus having been made, it must be met and sustained, if necessary, by the whole power of the navy and army." Private citizens called for arms to put down this obnoxious insurrection. A New

At 6 a.m. on January 9, the Sumter garrison heard cannon fire out in the harbor. The troops raced to their guns. Major Anderson, peering out to the harbor mouth, saw the *Star of the West* approaching, flying Old Glory. The ship was also spotted on Morris Island, where sat a South Carolina battery. One of the cannon, entrusted to gunner George E. Haynsworth, a cadet at The Citadel, fired two rounds. Haynsworth's aim was abominable, but arguably, those were the first shots of the Civil War.

Poor Anderson could not decide what to do. He merely stood on the parapet, excited and puzzled, watching the ship steam in. Then he and his officers saw the *Star* lower her flag and raise it again—obviously some sort of signal. But for what?

Fort Moultrie, manned by secessionists since the day after Anderson left, joined the shelling with its remounted guns. Anderson still took no action in support of the *Star;* he dithered about on the parapet, unable to

Yorker found it intolerable that "the nation pockets this insult to the national flag, a calm, dishonorable, vile submission." In turn, the talk of reprisal from the North played into the hands of the Southern fire-eaters, who urged the recalcitrant slave states to secede and close ranks for mutual defense.

Almost at once, a Mississippi convention voted 84 to 15 in favor of secession. "In an instant the hall was a scene of wild tumult," and amid deafening applause someone brought out an immense blue banner with a single white star, probably the inspiration of one of the South's most beloved patriotic songs, "The Bonnie Blue Flag." The next day, January 10, Florida joined Mississippi and South Carolina in secession, and a day later Alabama left the Union.

In addition to recording its grievances in its secession ordinance, Alabama became the first state formally to call for an affiliation of seceded states. "In order to frame a revisional as a permanent Government," the Alabama delegation declared, "the people of the States of Delaware, Maryland, Virginia, North Carolina, South Carolina, Florida, Georgia, Mississippi, Louisiana, Texas, Arkansas, Tennessee, Kentucky and Missouri, be and they are hereby invited to meet the people of the State of Alabama, by their delegates in convention, on the 4th day of February next in Montgomery." It was time to form a new nation.

On January 19, the state of Georgia joined the secession movement. Louisiana did the same a week later, and on February 1, Texas brought the number to seven. The United States was in chaos.

In Washington, on January 21, several congressmen and senators from the seceded states made farewell speeches and left their seats. Some used the occasion for a final stab at the Union, but others were obviously sorrowful. Mississippian Jefferson Davis declared in a voice quavering with emotion, "Whatever of offense there has been to me, I leave here. I carry with me no hostile remembrance. Whatever offense I have given, . . . I have, Senators, in this hour of our parting, to offer you my apology." Some wept as he spoke. There will be peace "if you so will it," he went on, but the North "may bring disaster on every part of the country, if you will have it thus." Should war come, "we will invoke the God of our fathers, who delivered them from the power of the lion, to protect us from the ravages of the bear." That night in his room as he prepared to travel home, Davis prayed for peace.

But the meager chances for peace were diminished steadily by Southern states in a bridge-burning mood. As each state passed its secession ordinance, it occupied or demanded the surrender of Federal arsenals and forts within its borders. On January 20, Mississippi forces seized Fort Massachusetts on Ship Island, a base for controlling the mouth of the Mississippi River. Georgia state troops took the Augusta arsenal on January 24, and two days later occupied the Federal works in Savannah. Even before seceding, the state took possession of strategic Fort Pulaski at the mouth of the Savannah River. Similarly, Louisiana took possession of Federal installations below New Orleans.

Only in Florida did the secessionists meet resistance. In command of Fort Barrancas, near Pensacola, was a young Union lieutenant, Adam Slemmer. Expecting to be attacked as soon as Florida seceded, Slemmer withdrew his tiny command of 46 men to Fort Pickens, situated on Santa Rosa Island at the mouth of Pensacola Bay. There later received some two dozen reinforcements from a Navy ship, and when Florida demanded his surrender on January 12, he refused. And when the Governors of both Florida and Alabama demanded that he turn over the fort, he impudently replied that "a governor is nobody here." Slemmer would again be supplied and reinforced without a shot being fired by either side; the Union flag would fly over his fort throughout the War. Meanwhile, Fort Taylor on Key West was

also garrisoned by Federals, providing the Union with another valuable base that served well in the years ahead.

Slemmer and brave Fort Pickens, however, brought the North only passing cheer in a secession winter that produced more and worse news every day. In February came a particularly galling affront: Brevet Major General David E. Twiggs—one of the four highest officers in the U.S. Army—eagerly surrendered military posts in Texas to the secessionists. Within days he was dismissed

from the service as a traitor, and he took such offense at the appellation that he wrote to Buchanan threatening to visit him "for the sole purpose of a personal interview"—the usual euphemism for a duel. It was an empty threat; Twiggs was 71 years old. Nevertheless, the incident gave ample warning that the Union must expect defections from the very army that would have to contest the growing insurrection.

For all practical purposes North and South passed the point of no return that February, when secessionist delegates meeting in Montgomery, Alabama, set up their Southern nation. From South Carolina came Robert Barnwell Rhett and former U.S. Senator James Chesnut, among others, and Georgia's delegation included its three foremost statesmen, Robert Toombs, Howell Cobb and Alexander H. Stephens. Most of the rest were Southern patriots little known outside their home states.

The delegates elected Cobb president of the convention. "The separation is perfect, complete, and perpetual," he told them. "The great duty is now imposed upon us of providing for these States a government for their future security and protection." Rarely had a revolutionary assembly acted with such speed and unanimity. On February 5, Christopher Memminger of South Carolina moved that the states form a new "confederacy," and was appointed head of a committee of 12 to begin working on a constitution. The committee reported back two days later, and on February 8 the Provisional Constitution of the Confederate States of America was adopted without dissent.

Predictably, the new charter did not differ greatly from that of the old Union; although these seceders tried to simplify the Constitution, they considered themselves the true constructionists and the Yankees the violators of the Constitution. Their temporary charter guaranteed the right to own slaves in any new territory but prohibited a resumption of the foreign slave trade. States were declared sovereign and independent; by implication, any state might even secede from the new nation. The President and Vice President would serve for six years and become ineligible for a second term.

With the easy adoption of this constitution, the delegates were faced with the critical task of choosing a leader. There was no time to arrange for a general election; that would come a year later when a permanent constitution was framed. The President had to be chosen here and now.

Who should lead them? The delegates of two states wanted Howell Cobb, though he did not seek the post. Among others considered for the post were blustery, hard-drinking Robert Toombs and quiet, somber Jefferson Davis. Both Toombs and Cobb suffered because they had made many enemies in their long careers. The decision was further simplified by a mistake Toombs made two days before the final vote. Alexander Stephens of Georgia, who was to become Vice President, wrote that Toombs "got quite tight at dinner and went to a party in town tighter than I ever saw him—too tight for his character and reputation by far. I think that evening's exhibition settled the Presidency where it fell."

With support for Toombs evaporating, the convention quickly voted for the man most acceptable to all factions, the man who had been neither too conservative nor too radical in the sectional crisis, the man who

could immediately present a unified front to the unseceded Southern states and the angry Northern states. Jefferson Davis was the man, and he would do.

While the convention discussed designs for a Confederate flag, word went out informing Davis of his selection. When the message reached him, he was helping his wife in the garden of Brierfield, their plantation near Vicksburg, Mississippi. Varina Davis saw his face pale as he read of his election. He said then, and would often repeat, that he had not wanted the office; rather, he had hoped for command of the Confederacy's army. Yet Davis, for all the faults that the coming years would reveal in him, was on balance the best available man for the job.

And thus at first, the Confederacy spoke

to the world in a moderate voice. On February 18, when Jefferson Davis took the oath of office as President of the Confederacy, he delivered a temperate inaugural address that sought to reassure both contentious sections. All the Southerners wanted, he told the North, was to be left alone. But if attacked, they would defend themselves, "and the suffering of millions will bear testimony to the folly and wickedness of our aggressors." Radicals like William L. Yancey began to feel better about this moderate when they heard those strong words. Many Northerners agreed with Davis' appeal for a peaceable separation and said of the seceded states, "Let the erring sisters go in peace."

Two weeks later another inaugural address was heard from a man even more committed to moderation. On March 4, 1861, Abraham Lincoln took his oath of office as the 16th President of the United States and addressed the South in conciliatory tones. He vowed to avoid war and at the same time to maintain the Union. He held that the Union was still whole, for it was by its nature indissoluble. He would enforce its laws and "hold, occupy, and possess" Federal property—meaning particularly Fort Sumter—but he would not initiate violent or aggressive action. "In your hands, my dissatisfied fellow-countrymen, and not in mine, is the momentous issue of civil war," he told them. "You can have no conflict without being yourselves the aggressors." He had sworn to defend the Union, and he would if he must, but surely the Southerners would not force his hand if they took time for reflection.

"I am loath to close," Lincoln said in a moving coda. "We are not enemies, but friends. We must not be enemies." Memories of the patriot days of the Revolution still bound them together. These fond sentiments would "swell the chorus of the Union, when again touched, as surely they will be, by the better angels of our nature."

But nothing President Lincoln could say made friends in the South. Emma Holmes of Charleston said that the speech was "just what was expected of him, stupid, ambiguous, vulgar and insolent," by virtue of which it "is everywhere considered as a virtual declaration of war."

Lincoln had been in office just one day when the simmering Sumter crisis boiled up again. With the U.S. mail and railroad service continuing to function more or less normally, a letter arrived from Major Anderson declaring that his position was nearly hopeless; that he needed 20,000 more troops to

President-elect Abraham Lincoln
raises the flag before a cheering
throng of Philadelphians at
Independence Hall on Washington's
birthday, 1861. "I don't think it
is Lincoln's person or character that
brings out the enthusiasm," wrote
a politician. "It must be the present
crisis of the country."

hold position in Charleston Harbor; that even if Sumter were not attacked, his dwindling food supply would soon force him to choose between starvation and surrender. In fact, the major's only hope had failed. He had bought plenty of time for reinforcements to be sent, but since none had arrived, the hiatus had worked out to the great advantage of the South Carolinians. They had sunk several old hulks in the harbor's main channel to impede any Federal attempt to relieve Sumter. And they had brought in many cannon seized from Federal arsenals and emplaced batteries to fire on Sumter from three sides.

It was not hard to detect in Anderson's woe-filled letter an unstated hope that he would be permitted to evacuate his garrison. But Lincoln, mindful of his public pledge to defend Federal property, solicited advice on the feasibility of reinforcing or resupplying Sumter. The counsel he received was more alarming than informative.

Lincoln's aggressive postmaster general, Montgomery Blair, was the only Cabinet member who shared the President's resolve to help Anderson hold Sumter. The opposition was led by William Seward, the disappointed presidential aspirant, whom Lincoln had appointed Secretary of State as a fence-mending gesture to the radical Eastern Republicans. The imperious New Yorker had decided that, with a little appeasement, the seceded Southern states would return peaceably to the Union fold, and he was deliberately creating the impression among associates that he, not the President, would set policy toward the secessionists—and, indeed, run the government. It did not help Lincoln that General Scott declared that Sumter could not be reinforced in time.

Lincoln acted first to prevent another

Sumter, approving an order that supplies be sent forthwith to Florida's Fort Pickens. And then, unwilling to accept Scott's adverse opinion, he told the general to send agents to Charleston to judge whether—and how—an expedition could relieve Sumter. Lincoln was sure to get the decision he wanted; Scott chose an agent known to be prejudiced in favor of a relief expedition. The man was Gustavus V. Fox, a former Navy captain, who for weeks had been telling everyone, including the press, that Fort Sumter could be and should be reinforced.

It boded ill for the Federals that the secessionists, too, knew exactly what Fox stood for. When the agent reached Charleston, he applied to the Confederates for permission to visit Sumter and report on its condition. Suspecting Fox but unwilling to send him packing, Confederates escorted him to the fort and tried to prevent his speaking privately with Major Anderson. With great difficulty Fox hinted to Anderson that a relief expedition was under discussion in Washington. But Anderson learned none of the details.

As Lincoln awaited word from Fox, a new batch of three commissioners from the Confederate States arrived in Washington to discuss foreign relations with Seward. The Secretary of State was too discreet to make Buchanan's mistake of meeting with the emissaries, but he agreed to advise them through an intermediary, Supreme Court Justice John A. Campbell, a Confederate collaborator, who was about to resign from the bench and head south. On March 15, without confiding his plans to anyone, Seward told Campbell that Sumter would be evacuated soon—in fact, within three days.

Campbell and the Confederate diplomats were ecstatic; it seemed they had won with-

Jefferson Davis (*above*) is sworn in as President of the Confederate States of America on the capitol steps at Montgomery, Alabama, on February 18, 1861. "The audience was large and brilliant," he wrote to his wife. "Upon my weary heart was showered smiles, plaudits and flowers, but beyond them, I saw trouble and thorns innumerable."

out firing a shot. But six days went by and brought no word that Sumter had been abandoned. Seward, still cocky on March 21, reassured Campbell, and again the Confederates were mollified. Then came March 29 and a decision. Lincoln held a Cabinet meeting. Reports from his agents in Charleston, especially Gustavus Fox, advised that Sumter could be resupplied. And by then most of the Cabinet members had changed their views, goaded by Northern Republicans who were furious that nothing was being done. Seward found that he was suddenly all alone on the side of evacuation. Lincoln ordered that an expedition be assembled to relieve Sumter as soon as possible.

Now Seward, squirming to avoid the consequences of his folly, made matters worse by sending Lincoln a letter full of wild proposals. He suggested that the United States provoke war with either Spain or France in the expectation that the South would reunite with the North against the common foe, and he advised the President to let him take over the onerous chore of running the government. Lincoln had ample cause for dismissing Seward out of hand. But he admired Seward's abilities and expected to win his loyalty. He ignored Seward's letter.

On April 4, Lincoln informed Major Anderson by ordinary mail that the expedition was coming, but not when. Captain Fox,

A crowd of 30,000 watches the inauguration of Abraham Lincoln as the 16th President of the United States on the 4th of March, 1861. Sharpshooters were posted in the windows of the Capitol to guard against assassination attempts by Southern sympathizers.

who was to lead the mission as an unofficial representative of the President, had planned for an eight-ship fleet, but he was forced to compete for the few available vessels with officers arranging a relief expedition to Fort Pickens. Since Lincoln still hoped to avert a clash over Sumter, he ordered Fox to send ashore supplies only, no reinforcements—unless the Confederates attacked him or interfered with his mission. The President then sent a messenger with a letter to Governor Pickens, telling him of this strictly limited mission and stressing its peaceful intent.

The Governor, suspecting perfidy, rushed the letter to President Davis in Montgomery and alerted the Confederate commander at Charleston, a handsome, dapper Louisiana Frenchman named Pierre Gustave Toutant Beauregard. The brigadier general needed no special urging. But he was undoubtedly bemused by one of those poignant ironies that often crop up in wartime. While Beauregard was at West Point in the late 1830s, he had studied artillery under an instructor who became his friend and was now his adversary, Major Anderson. It appeared that he would have to recite his lessons to Anderson from the mouths of his cannon.

Beauregard had worked feverishly to complete his artillery build-up around the harbor. By early April he already had brought overwhelming strength to bear on Fort Sumter. Fort Moultrie on Sullivan's Island had three 8-inch, long-range cannon called columbiads, two 8-inch high-trajectory howitzers, five smoothbores that fired 32-pound shot and four 24-pounders. Deployed outside Moultrie's walls were five squat, wide-mouthed 10-inch mortars, designed expressly to reduce fortifications, and also two 32-pounders, two 24-pounders and a 9-inch

Brigadier General Pierre G. T.
Beauregard, commander of
Confederate forces confronting
Fort Sumter, was a handsome man—
and allegedly vain about it. When
his black hair began turning white in
1861, friends blamed the burden
of command, but cynics had another
explanation: The Union sea blockade
had cut off the import of hair dyes.

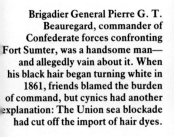

Dahlgren smoothbore, a lightweight gun that could fire a heavy charge. Soon to be moored off the west end of Sullivan's Island was an ungainly construction called the Floating Battery—two 42-pounders and two 32-pounders mounted on a raft and protected by iron shielding.

On James Island west of Sumter, Fort Johnson had a 24-pounder and four 10-inch mortars. And at the tip of Morris Island, immediately south of Sumter, stood seven 10-inch mortars, two 42-pounders, an English Blakely rifled cannon and the Ironclad Battery, so called because its three 8-inch columbiads were protected front and top by a wooden shield faced with heavy iron bars.

To man these guns and to storm Sumter if necessary, Beauregard had roughly 6,000 men of all ages and degrees of training. Established militia companies had been called out and marched into Charleston to welcom-

ing cannon salutes. Fuzz-cheeked boys had run away from home to bear arms against Sumter. A few old men, most notably the veteran crusader for secession Edmund Ruffin, came to take a hand in the great event.

Augustus Dickert, a 15-year-old militiaman who had hurried to Charleston fearing that the war would be over before he could get into it, wrote that "everyone was in a high glee—palmetto cockades, brass buttons, uniforms, and gaudy epaulettes were seen in every direction." The town was "ablaze with excitement, flags waved from the house tops, the heavy tread of the embryo soldiers could be heard in the streets, the corridors of hotels, and in all the public places." Southern patriots, even those "who were as ignorant and as much strangers to manual labor as though they had been infants," moved guns and dug emplacements until their hands were blistered and bloodied. By the end of the first week of April, Beauregard was ready and more than ready.

So was the Confederate government in Montgomery. Well before Lincoln's April 6 message arrived in the Alabama capital, the secessionists were tired of waiting and bitter over Seward's apparent duplicity—and therefore, presumably, Lincoln's. With Lincoln's message in hand, Jefferson Davis convened his Cabinet on April 9. Lincoln had maneuvered the Confederates into the position he had promised in his inaugural: There would be no first shot unless they fired it. Davis did not want that shot fired any more than Lincoln did. Yet after all the months of anxiety and indecision, the firing of that shot seemed less dreadful than before, a release and a climax that many Confederates demanded. A friend of Davis' warned him, "Unless you sprinkle blood in the face of the

Southern people they will be back in the old Union in less than ten days."

There was a likelier eventuality—that if the Confederate government did not act, South Carolina might do so on its own, undermining the new and untested authority of the Confederate States. All but one of the Cabinet members favored ordering Beauregard to go ahead and open fire. The exception was Secretary of State Robert Toombs. He counseled caution and warned that "the firing upon that fort will inaugurate a civil war greater than any the world has yet seen."

That was a risk that the Cabinet was prepared to take. On April 10, Secretary of War Leroy Pope Walker telegraphed Beauregard that he was to demand Sumter's immediate evacuation; if he was refused for any reason, he was to "proceed in such manner as you may determine, to reduce it."

That night in Charleston, the excitement and patriotic passions that had been building up since secession last December reached fever pitch. All night long parades snaked through the streets, drums rolled and horses' hooves clattered, great bonfires cast leaping shadows. Those Southerners who still treasured the Union did not dare to speak their minds. Even Southern patriots who were satisfied by the current peaceable progress of the Confederate States were swept aside in the hysteria of the moment.

This was no place for moderation, no time for trepidation. Charleston was in the hands of the fire-eaters; former Unionist Michael P. O'Connor called the Union "a dead carcass stinking in the nostrils of the Southern people." The night belonged to Roger Pryor who, from the balcony of his hotel, spoke as a Virginian to the seething crowd of South Carolinians in the street below.

"I thank you especially," Pryor shouted, "that you have at last annihilated this accursed Union, reeking with corruption and insolent with excess of tyranny. Not only is it gone, but gone forever.

"As sure as tomorrow's sun will rise upon us, just so sure will old Virginia be a member of the Southern Confederacy; and I will tell your Governor what will put her in the Southern Confederacy in less than an hour by a Shrewsbury clock.

"Strike a blow!" Pryor cried. "The very moment that blood is shed, old Virginia will make common cause with her sisters of the South."

The final day of peace, April 11, 1861, dawned warm and overcast in Charleston. Many people sensed that the long Sumter crisis would end this day, and their giddy expectancy increased hour by hour. Mary Boykin Chesnut, whose husband, James, now served as a colonel on Beauregard's staff, was as much a Southern patriot as anyone; but she did not share the radicals' passion for war, and she feared that war was just an inch away. "And so we fool on," she wrote in her diary, "into the black cloud ahead of us."

Putting aside her fears, Mrs. Chesnut that noon enjoyed "the merriest, maddest dinner we have had yet." By tacit agreement there was no talk of war at her table, but thoughts of war stirred the men's blood and loosened their tongues. Mary Chesnut noted that the men were "more audaciously wise and witty" than usual, and "for once in my life I listened." Then came a signal development.

Before noon, James Chesnut was summoned by General Beauregard. The colonel was given a written surrender ultimatum to

Confederate forces at Cummings Point on Morris Island prepare to bombard Fort Sumter in these on-the-spot sketches by William Waud, an artist for Frank Leslie's *Illustrated Newspaper*. At left, slaves mount a heavy gun. At bottom, soldiers unload supplies from rafts while engineers use palmetto logs to erect earthworks and emplace guns behind protective iron rails.

139

deliver to Major Anderson. Accompanied by Colonel James A. Chisholm and Captain Stephen D. Lee, Chesnut was rowed out to Fort Sumter, and there he presented his message to the Federal commander.

Anderson withdrew to discuss the ultimatum with his officers. They all agreed to reject it. Anderson wrote out his response and handed the note to Chesnut. Then as he strolled to the wharf to see the Confederates off, the major asked Chesnut, "Will General Beauregard open his batteries without further notice to me?"

"I think not," replied Chesnut. "No, I can say to you that he will not, without further notice."

"I shall await the first shot," Anderson said, then added quietly, "and if you do not batter us to pieces, we shall be starved out in a few days."

Returning to Charleston, Chesnut reported Anderson's hint to Beauregard. At once

the general told Secretary Walker that they might get the prize without a shot simply by waiting until Sumter's provisions ran out. Walker replied that he did not "desire needlessly to bombard Fort Sumter," and if Anderson would state the date when he would evacuate, Beauregard could hold his fire. Beauregard composed a last message to Anderson and summoned Chesnut to deliver it. Chesnut was empowered to act on the spot according to Anderson's response.

Just before 1 a.m. on April 12, Chesnut and his party, this time accompanied by Roger Pryor, again approached Fort Sumter. Pryor stayed in the boat while the others delivered the message.

Again Anderson withdrew with his officers to discuss their response. They debated for three hours—so long that Chesnut concluded that they were deliberately stalling and interrupted them to hasten their answer.

Finally, shortly after 3 a.m. on April 12,

The opening shot of the Civil War, a shell fired from Fort Johnson (*far left*), explodes over Fort Sumter at 4:30 a.m. on April 12, 1861, signaling Confederate batteries to start their bombardment. Tracking the shell by its burning fuse, a South Carolina gunner on Morris Island (*foreground*, said it looked "like a firefly."

Anderson handed the envoys his response. He would evacuate on April 15, he said, holding his fire in the meantime unless fired upon, or unless he detected some act of hostile intent that would endanger the fort. Further, his agreement to hold fire might be altered if he received other instructions from his government, "or additional supplies."

Chesnut decided that Anderson was allowing himself too many ways out, offering terms that were "manifestly futile." So Chesnut wrote out a formal declaration. By Beauregard's authority, it read, "we have the honor to notify you that he will open the fire of his batteries on Fort Sumter in one hour."

It was 3:30 a.m. Anderson escorted the Confederates back to their boat and shook hands with each one. "If we never meet in this world again," he said in farewell, "God grant that we may meet in the next."

The bells of St. Michael's in Charleston were pealing 4 a.m. as Chesnut's party rowed up to Fort Johnson. Chesnut ordered Captain George S. James to fire the signal shell that would open the bombardment at 4:30.

Everyone was waiting. Roger Pryor was offered the honor of firing the signal gun. But he had dire second thoughts: "I could not fire the first gun of the war," he said. When Captain James gave the order to fire, it was Lieutenant Henry S. Farley who jerked the lanyard that sent the signal shell arcing high into the sky over Fort Sumter.

Mary Chesnut was lying awake in her Charleston hotel room when that first shell burst. "I sprang out of bed," she wrote. "And on my knees—prostrate—I prayed as I never prayed before."

It was too late. Now no one could stem the tide of events—not Anderson or Beauregard, not Lincoln or Davis. America had gone out of control.

West Pointers at the Crossroads

In the autumn of 1860, the 1,108 officers of the United States Army were scattered across the nation on garrison duty in forts along the coast or in the new Western territories. The news in November of Abraham Lincoln's election sent a shock wave through the ranks. Secession now loomed, and the officers from the South faced a wrenching decision: to remain loyal to the Union or to resign their commissions and defect to the Southern cause.

A good index of how the officer corps chose sides can be found in the West Point class of 1857. Thirty-six of the 38 graduates of this class—the first class to pose for graduation photographs—appear below and on the following pages according to their allegiance and academic ranking. The missing pair were John T. Magruder, who died in 1859, and Marcus A. Reno (later important in the Indian wars), who failed to show up for the picture-taking session. For most of these men, the choice was clear: They went the way of their home states. In fact, about 40 per cent of the class "went South," in the vernacular of the day.

The U.S. Army brass, fearing mass defection by Southern officers, tried to bribe the Southerners to remain loyal.

Defenders of the Confederacy

RICHARD K. MEADE, VIRGINIA
Engineer, North Carolina;
died of disease, July 1862; Major.

E. PORTER ALEXANDER, GEORGIA
Chief of Artillery, Longstreet's
Corps; Brigadier General.

WILLIAM P. SMITH, VIRGINIA
Chief of Engineers under Gene
Early, Army of the Valley; Colo

GEORGE E. CUNNINGHAM, ALABAMA
Commanded 51st Virginia Infantry,
then artillery in N.C.; Colonel.

HENRY C. McNEILL, TEXAS
Served on General Sibley's staff;
Colonel of the 5th Texas Cavalry.

AURELIUS F. CONE, GEORGIA
Assistant Quartermaster General in
Virginia; Lieutenant Colonel.

PAUL J. QUATTLEBAUM, S. CAROL
Commanded artillery in the defen
Mobile, Ala.; Lieutenant Colon

E. Porter Alexander (*below*) was offered a tour of duty on the West Coast, far from the likely theaters of war. This, he was told, would spare him the anguish of raising his sword against his native state of Georgia, his family and his friends.

Alexander refused and became one of four cadets in the class of 1857 to resign upon learning that his home state had seceded from the Union. Eleven other Southerners in the class defected to the Confederate officer corps after hostilities commenced at Fort Sumter on April 12, 1861. Three of these men—Richard K. Meade, Manning M. Kimmel and Lafayette Peck—did not join the Confederate Army until they had seen service against the South. Meade, a second lieutenant from Virginia, was in the Fort Sumter garrison during the bombardment and later surrendered to Confederate forces under General P.G.T. Beauregard. One of Meade's West Point classmates, Samuel W. Ferguson, was the Confederate lieutenant who hoisted the Rebel flag over the fort.

During the War, the classmates of '57 served with distinction on both sides; highlights of their service records and their highest career ranks appear here below their pictures. Four Confederate and six Union officers rose to the rank of general or its honorary equivalent, brevet general. By the end of the War, seven of the classmates would be dead, killed in battle or victims of wounds or illness.

THOMAS J. BERRY, GEORGIA
Commanded the 60th Georgia Infantry; Lieutenant Colonel.

OLIVER H. FISH, KENTUCKY
Instructor; died New Liberty, Ky., February 1865; Second Lieutenant.

SAMUEL W. FERGUSON, S. CAROLINA
Commanded a cavalry brigade, W. H. Jackson's Division; Brig. General.

MANNING M. KIMMEL, MISSOURI
Union officer at First Bull Run; joined the Confederacy; Major.

JOHN S. MARMADUKE, MISSOURI
[com]manded cavalry under General [Pric]e; captured 1864; Major General.

GEORGE W. HOLT, ALABAMA
Staff officer to Generals Stephen D. Lee and Nathan B. Forrest; Major.

ROBERT H. ANDERSON, GEORGIA
Brigade commander, Wheeler's Cavalry Corps; Brigadier General.

LAFAYETTE PECK, TENNESSEE
Instructor; died of disease in Alabama, 1864; Lieutenant.

Loyalists for the Union

JOHN C. PALFREY, MASSACHUSETTS
Chief Engineer, 13th Corps; Brevet
Brigadier General.

HENRY M. ROBERT, OHIO
Chief Engineer of the defenses of
Philadelphia; Captain.

GEORGE C. STRONG, MASSACHUSE
Mortally wounded at Fort Wagn
S.C., July 1863; Major Genera

CHARLES H. MORGAN, NEW YORK
Chief of Artillery and Chief of Staff,
2nd Corps; Brigadier General.

ABRAM C. WILDRICK, NEW JERSEY
Colonel, 39th New Jersey Infantry;
Brevet Brigadier General.

CHARLES J. WALKER, KENTUCK
Commanded 10th Ky. Cavalry; C
of Cavalry, 23rd Corps; Colone

GEORGE H. WEEKS, MAINE
Chief Quartermaster, 3rd Corps;
Brevet Lieutenant Colonel.

IRA W. CLAFLIN, IOWA
Captain, 6th U.S. Cavalry; wounded
at Funkstown, Md.; Brevet Major.

JOSEPH S. CONRAD, NEW YORK
Wounded at Wilson's Creek,
Missouri; Lieutenant Colonel, S

J. L. KIRBY SMITH, NEW YORK
43rd Ohio Infantry; mortally
~~ounded, October 1862; Colonel.

THOMAS G. BAYLOR, VIRGINIA
On staff of General Sherman in
Atlanta Campaign; Brevet Colonel.

HALDIMAND PUTNAM, NEW HAMPSHIRE
7th N.H. Infantry; killed at Fort
Wagner, S.C., July 1863; Colonel.

GEORGE A. KENSEL, KENTUCKY
Artillery Chief of Department of the
Gulf; Brevet Colonel.

FRANCIS BEACH, CONNECTICUT
~~6th Conn. Infantry; captured at
~~nouth, N.C., April 1864; Colonel.

WILLIAM SINCLAIR, OHIO
Commanded 6th Pennsylvania
Reserves; twice wounded; Colonel.

AUGUSTUS G. ROBINSON, MAINE
Captain in Quartermaster General's
Office, Washington; Brevet Major.

EDWARD R. WARNER, PENNSYLVANIA
Inspector of Artillery, Army of the
Potomac; Brevet Brigadier General.

~~WARD J. CONNER, NEW HAMPSHIRE
~~ U.S. Infantry; retired because of
~~ness, December 1863; Captain.

GEORGE RYAN, CONNECTICUT
140th N.Y.; killed at Spotsylvania,
Virginia, May 1864; Colonel.

CHARLES E. FARRAND, NEW YORK
11th U.S. Infantry; captured
at Corinth, Miss., 1862; Captain.

THOMAS J. LEE, INDIANA
Resigned commission, 1859; served
as private, 1863-1865.

145

The Guns Have Spoken

"Civil War is actually upon us, and strange to say, it brings a feeling of relief: the suspense is over."

SENATOR JOHN SHERMAN OF OHIO

Sergeant James Chester and several Federal soldiers were standing in the dark on the ramparts of Fort Sumter when, at 4:30 a.m. or soon thereafter, the Confederate signal shot came from Morris Island. Chester later wrote: "The eyes of the watchers easily detected and followed the burning fuse which marked the course of the shell as it mounted among the stars."

Almost at once the Confederate batteries all around Fort Sumter commenced firing, "and shot and shell went screaming over Sumter as if an army of devils were swooping around it." For a while the Union soldiers coolly stood in place making professional remarks on how the Confederate fire was too high. But "in a few minutes the novelty disappeared," and so did the Federals, who continued their discussions in the safety of the fort's interior.

Thus began a fight that bore practically no resemblance to the cruel headlong battles that came later. It was a strange, tentative, melodramatic fight. Both sides would make absurd mistakes—the natural result of inexperience. Both sides would sweat and strain to follow the rules of war, to prove themselves responsible and honorable men. Yet this sense of decorum went deeper than mere Victorian punctilio. Men who had hotly demanded war now drew back, shaken to find themselves facing an American enemy. It was as if the start of hostilities renewed, however briefly, the affection countrymen felt for one another.

Where did the first Confederate shot hit Fort Sumter? The men of the garrison later debated that question with great vehemence. Captain Abner Doubleday swore that it "struck the wall of the magazine where I was lying, penetrated the masonry, and burst very near my head." Smoke poured into the room through the magazine's ventilation shafts, and for an instant Doubleday thought that the magazine had caught fire. But he soon satisfied himself that there was no fire and stubbornly remained in bed, refusing to be disturbed by the mere commencement of war.

When the first sounds of firing reached Charleston, every bed emptied. Wrote Mary Chesnut in her hotel room: "There was a sound of stir all over the house, pattering of feet in the corridor—all seemed hurrying one way." In the darkness before dawn, the citizens raced to their rooftops or the Battery waterfront and watched the shells exploding. From her own vantage point on the roof of the hotel, Mrs. Chesnut reported that "the women were wild, there on the housetop"; they cried or prayed while the men stood yelling their encouragement to the Confederate gunners. The tension was oppressive for many. "I knew my husband was rowing about in a boat somewhere in that dark bay," wrote Mary Chesnut. "And who could tell what each volley accomplished of death and destruction?" So distressed was she that she sat down for a moment on something that looked like a black

In a banked headline for April 13, 1861, the St. Paul, Minnesota, *Pioneer and Democrat* tells a terse story of the bombardment of Fort Sumter and the start of the War.

stool. "Get up, you foolish woman—your dress is on fire!" shouted a man. She had sat on a chimney.

For more than two hours, the men of Fort Sumter made no effort to answer the bombardment. At 6 a.m. the enlisted men assembled for reveille in the bombproofs inside the walls. After the roll call, the men went to breakfast; most of them considered the meal a grim joke, for there was nothing left to eat except salt pork, which Sergeant Chester and others found "very rusty indeed." Their officers fared a bit better, swallowing a little farina and some rice.

Only after his men had finished their spartan meal did Major Anderson turn his attention to the bombardment. He had to decide whether to return fire and, if so, how. His biggest and most effective guns were mounted on the top level of the fort, the barbette tier. Chief among the 26 cannon up there were eight heavy columbiads of various sizes and four 8-inch howitzers. These weapons could do important damage to the Confederate batteries now assailing him. The trouble was that the big guns were out in the open, and they afforded no protection for the crews manning them.

Anderson decided that it was too risky to use the barbette guns. That left the 21 working guns sheltered in the vaulted masonry casemates on the fort's lower level. These cannon, 32- and 42-pounders, could be deadly against approaching ships, but they were much less effective against masonry and earthworks. For yet another problem, the Federals had no fuses for their explosive shells and would be able to fire nothing but solid shot.

So Anderson concluded that he could fight only a defensive battle. He would open a counterfire, of course. But he would be judicious about it; he would conserve his munitions and his manpower and defend the flag until Captain Gustavus Fox's relief expedition arrived. If the fort received enough men and supplies, he could continue to hold out no matter how much iron the Confederates threw at him.

At about 6:30, the drummer beat assembly and the garrison lined up once more in the bombproofs. Heading the force with Anderson were nine other officers, five of whom would become generals in the course of the War. In this first clash, they commanded 68 soldiers, eight musicians and 43 civilian workmen who were under no obligation to fight. Anderson's orders to the garrison were brief and explicit. "Be careful of your lives," he advised his troops. "Do your duty coolly, determinedly and cautiously. Indiscretion is not valor."

Anderson had decided that the gun crews would man the cannon in four-hour shifts. Commanding the first relief team was Abner Doubleday, the senior captain; he assigned his detail to a battery of 32-pounders that bore directly on Cummings Point, where the Ironclad Battery and other Confederate units were firing away furiously. On Doubleday's left, a lieutenant named Jefferson C. Davis led his crews to guns aimed at the Confederate batteries on James Island. And surgeon Samuel Crawford, who was also a competent artilleryman, joined a third party on the opposite side of the fort and manned the guns that aimed toward Fort Moultrie and the Floating Battery.

It was Doubleday who, at about 7 o'clock, delightedly fired the first Union shot. "In aiming the first gun fired against the rebellion," he declared later, "I had no feeling of

147

Nine Union officers in command of the Fort Sumter garrison were photographed before the Confederate bombardment. Seated left to right are Captain Abner Doubleday, Major Robert Anderson, Assistant Surgeon Samuel W. Crawford and Captain J. G. Foster. Those standing are (*from left*) Captain Truman Seymour, Lieutenant George W. Snyder, Lieutenant Jefferson C. Davis, Second Lieutenant Richard K. Meade and Lieutenant Theodore Talbot. Six of the officers eventually rose to the rank of general.

self-reproach, for I fully believed that the contest was inevitable, and was not of our seeking." It was simply a matter of good and evil, he believed, "a contest, politically speaking, as to whether virtue or vice should rule." This was the great moment in Doubleday's career. Though he rose to the rank of major general, he was never a distinguished general, and his latter-day fame as the man who "invented" the game of baseball rested on pure fabrication; he never had a thing to do with developing the sport.

Doubleday's shot was a miss. According to Captain George Cuthbert, whose Palmetto Guard was manning the Ironclad Battery, "The ball passed a few feet above the upper bolts of the shed." The Confederates were enormously relieved by that first shot. Ex-

plained old Edmund Ruffin, who was busily firing his own cannon: "I was fearful that Major Anderson did not intend to fire at all. It would have cheapened our conquest of the fort, if effected, if no hostile defense had been made—and still more increased the disgrace of failure."

Ruffin was pleased to note that the inexperienced Confederate gunners were rapidly learning their trade: "The proportion of effective balls and shells increased with the practice." After a while the white-haired Virginian wandered among the several batteries on Cummings Point and occasionally accepted the honor of jerking a lanyard. There Ruffin saw eight or 10 men running at full speed along the shore, and he thought at first that they were fleeing from a position that was taking Yankee hits. On the contrary, as he later observed, "they were running after spent balls, to secure them as memorials or trophies."

In fact, those cannonballs were but a few of the many misses by Doubleday's guns. In the full four hours of his first shift, only seven of his shots hit the works of the Ironclad Battery, and all of them bounced off the iron sheathing without doing much damage. Doubleday was happy to turn the guns over to Captain Truman Seymour and his relief party when the shift ended.

"Doubleday, what in the world is the matter here, and what is all this uproar about?" asked Seymour facetiously.

In the same vein Doubleday responded, "There is a trifling difference of opinion between us and our neighbors opposite, and we are trying to settle it."

Lieutenant Davis' guns fared no better than Doubleday's against the batteries on James Island; the cannonballs buried themselves in the sand in front of the palmetto-log Confederate breastworks. And surgeon Crawford became thoroughly frustrated in his attempts to damage the Floating Battery off Sullivan's Island. The shots that his gunners aimed at the roof of the battery bounced off harmlessly, and the shots that they tried to scale across the water and into the battery's vulnerable water line were blocked by

Union soldier John Carmody, a lone daredevil who ignored orders against firing the dangerously exposed cannon atop Fort Sumter, watches a shot hit home before dashing along the rampart to fire the next gun.

a sea wall. Yet Crawford also discovered that the Floating Battery, so much feared in the previous weeks, was not very effective either. As a result, the surgeon received Anderson's permission to shift his gun crews to three other cannon that bore directly on Fort Moultrie. In this assignment Crawford finally tasted success. Although his men failed to silence a single Moultrie gun, they did manage to inflict considerable damage on the wooden structures in and around the fort, pelting the Confederate forces there with flying splinters of wood.

Noontime found Sumter withstanding the bombardment fairly well. The outer walls of the fort were virtually impervious to the enemy round shot, and only the mortar shells lobbed into the enclosed parade ground did any real damage. Explosions here had severely damaged the adjacent barracks, and there was danger of a fire near the main powder magazine.

The men were holding up better than the fort. They had been penned in here for three and a half months, undernourished, inactive and depressed by their confinement. But under fire they performed with vigor and alacrity. So did the civilian workmen; some vol-

A map of Charleston Harbor pinpoints Fort Sumter's strategic location, shows the position and range of the surrounding Confederate batteries, and lists the cannon available to both sides.

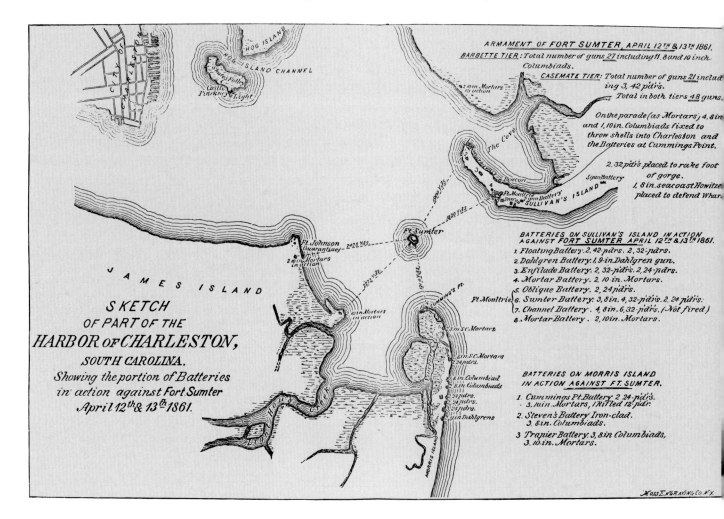

untarily carried ammunition, while others began sewing rags and clothing into additional cartridge bags for gunpowder charges. Anderson had every reason to be pleased with his command.

A few spirited soldiers did disobey the major's injunction against taking needless risks. The big columbiads that could do such interesting damage to the Confederates were sitting loaded and unmanned on the barbette tier. Although Anderson had declared that level to be off-limits, a soldier by the name of John Carmody could not put temptation behind him. After hours of the shelling,

he furtively made his way to the barbette, found the guns aimed at Fort Moultrie and fired them one after another. "The contest," wrote Sergeant Chester, "was merely Carmody against the Confederate States." But by himself Carmody was unable to reload the giant guns with 65-pound and 100-pound balls, and once he had fired them all he was forced to retire.

On the other side of the fort, two sergeants imitated Carmody's escapade. They manned one of the 10-inch columbiads facing Morris Island and fired a massive shot that barely missed the Ironclad Battery. Then, with

Wreathed in the smoke of battle, Fort Sumter exchanges fire with Confederate guns in an engraving from *Le Monde Illustré* of Paris. The long apex of Sumter's pentagon points toward Fort Moultrie on Sullivan's Island; Charleston is barely visible at upper left.

enormous effort, they managed to reload the gun with its 100-pound projectile. Their feat, together with Carmody's, persuaded the Confederates that the barbette guns were henceforth going to be used, so their gunners started to concentrate on Fort Sumter's upper level. Their fire soon became, according to Sergeant Chester, "a perfect hurricane of shot."

Anderson could scarcely have failed to notice the disobedience of Carmody and friends, but the major had more important matters to worry about. When the bombardment began, Fort Sumter had only 700 cloth gunpowder cartridges. The gunplay of the morning had severely reduced that supply, and the workmen sewing more bags were falling steadily behind. So, to avoid running out of cartridges even temporarily, Anderson shut down all but two guns firing on Cummings Point, two on Fort Moultrie and another two on the Sullivan's Island batteries. This way he could sustain at least a show of resistance.

An added problem was the constant danger of fire. The Sumter barracks had been faced with brick, supposedly to make them fireproof, but the Confederates made use of a proven countertactic. Some of the batteries placed cannonballs in a heavy-duty oven and heated them red-hot before firing them. These "hot shot" lodged inside the barracks and set the wood aflame. At mid-morning, a fire started on one of the upper floors. It had hardly been extinguished when another one broke out. Three times that day flames spread through the barracks. Oddly enough, one of the fires was put out by a Confederate shot; it ruptured a water tank and drowned the blaze.

And always on the major's mind was the relief expedition. Would it arrive in time? He kept a lookout stationed at a seaward embrasure, but the hours slipped by and there was no sign of the ships. It was not until about 1 o'clock in the afternoon that the first vessels of Fox's relief expedition were sighted beyond the bar at the harbor mouth. The garrison cheered and Anderson delightedly dipped Sumter's flag to signal the ships that the fort was all right.

Fox, aboard the steamer *Baltic*, had arrived at his specified rendezvous at about 3 a.m. that morning. Though he expected to meet seven other vessels there, he found that only the cutter *Harriet Lane* had beaten him to the rendezvous, and three hours passed before the sloop *Pawnee* appeared. Two other sloops, the *Powhatan* and the *Pocahontas*, as well as three tugs for landing supplies, still had not shown up by 6 a.m. Though Fox did not know it, the *Powhatan* would never arrive; she had been diverted to Florida to hold Fort Pickens. And none of the tugs would show up in time.

Not long after 6 o'clock, Fox decided against waiting any longer for the two sloops. He could not see or hear from the distance that the fort was under attack, and so, obedient to his orders to land only supplies unless he was opposed, Fox took just the *Baltic* and the *Harriet Lane* in toward Sumter. But as soon as he saw and heard the intense bombardment, he put back out to inform the Naval officers on board the *Pawnee*. The officers worked out a plan to wait until nightfall and then send in a few boatloads of supplies in the darkness. Fox opposed the plan at first. But, considering the continued absence of the two warships, he was persuaded to wait for the *Powhatan* to arrive. Then the *Pawnee* and the *Harriet*

Lane would defy the shore batteries and accompany the *Baltic* in to Sumter.

The rest of the afternoon passed without change: The Confederates maintained their fire, Anderson kept up his token resistance and Fox lurked expectantly out beyond the harbor. Around 7 p.m. a sudden rainstorm came up and extinguished the last sparks of Sumter's barracks fire, and at the same time Anderson ordered his command to cease firing for the night. The Confederates reduced their fire, too; only the 10-inch mortars were left in action, and each one lobbed only four shells an hour into Sumter.

That evening Anderson ordered Lieutenant George W. Snyder to survey the damage to the fort. Snyder completed his tour of inspection with Crawford, and what they discovered was not particularly pretty. An 8-inch cannonball fired 1,250 yards at relatively low velocity from an unrifled cannon would penetrate brick masonry no more than 11 inches. But the masonry walls on all five sides of Sumter, especially the wall facing Moultrie, were deeply cratered. In one place, repeated shots striking a small area had carved out a cavity some 20 inches deep, and Crawford concluded that sooner or later the bombardment would breach the wall. The main gate, too, was damaged, and the parapet had been heavily battered, with its chimneys knocked down, its stair towers de-

From the Battery at Charleston Harbor, 5,000 soldiers and civilians watch the bombardment of Fort Sumter on the morning of April 13, 1861. As flame and smoke engulfed the Federal bastion, many women spectators wept for its defenders.

stroyed and its guns dismounted. Crawford reported that the fort "presented a picture of havoc and ruin." But Sumter could easily continue fighting.

The exhausted Federals slept as best they could that night. But the men on guard kept up a sharp watch for the relief boats and also for a Confederate attempt to storm the fort in the darkness. They suddenly realized that the possibility of confusion was dreadful in a war between Americans. An attack force as well as reinforcements would come by boat and would answer any challenge in English. "It would be horrible to fire upon friends," said Sergeant Chester, yet "it would be fatal not to fire upon enemies."

On the morning of April 13, Anderson's men breakfasted on a little salt pork and some rice, and then, grumbling because Captain Fox had failed to arrive, went back to their guns to answer Beauregard's bombardment. Anderson decided to concentrate his fire on Fort Moultrie, the only target he was damaging. But once again the arsenal's dwindling supply of cartridges forced him to cut back his rate of fire to only one round every 10 minutes.

Now, more Confederate gunners were firing hot shot. Time and time again the barracks caught fire and the men doused the flames. But by 10 a.m. the fire was raging nearly out of control, and the mortar shells exploding in the parade ground made any attempts at fire fighting extremely hazardous. Anderson ordered the men to let the blaze run its course.

By noon the fort was burning wherever there was wood to catch fire. The entire officers' section was aflame. The fire spread to the wooden main gate and devoured most of it. And all the while, the flames crept closer to the 300 barrels of powder stored in the magazine, unwisely established near a wooden barracks.

Anderson put every available man to work removing the powder. It was perilous work, for much powder had been spilled in ribbons the day before, and if the loose stuff ignited, fire might race to the magazine. And of course, the Confederate shells plunging into the parade ground could just as easily dispatch the exposed men as they rolled the barrels to safety in the masonry casemate.

One officer said the men moved 96 barrels. Others thought only 50 or so were removed. In any case, the fire got so close that Anderson stopped the barrel-moving operation and ordered that the coppper-sheathed door be closed. He could only hope that the magazine would not blow.

By this time, the smoke billowing from the blaze had penetrated to every part of the fort. "We came very near being stifled with the dense livid smoke from the burning buildings," an officer later remembered. "The men lay prostrate on the ground, with wet handkerchiefs over their mouths and eyes, gasping for breath." Some of the soldiers clambered outside the gun embrasures, braving the Confederate cannon fire just to breathe clear air.

Flying cinders presented another threat. At any moment they might ignite the loose gunpowder and explode the moved barrels or the 9-inch shells that Anderson had hidden up on the parapet and in the stair towers, to be used as grenades in the event of an assault. Indeed, the flying sparks did detonate a pile of grenades just as Crawford started up to the parapet to search for the fleet. The whole stair tower exploded. The surgeon had to fight his way through rubble to

Union gunners in a Fort Sumter casemate work their cannon under the watchful eye of Major Robert Anderson, the garrison commander. Some of the gunners peer through the embrasure to determine where their last shot has landed.

In this contemporary engraving, a Confederate battery pounds away at a flaming Fort Sumter. The Rebel gunner felled by Union fire (*center foreground*) was a figment of the artist's imagination; in reality, no one on either side was killed or seriously wounded during the siege.

reach the top, and from there he could see the ships riding the wind-whipped waves exactly where they had been the evening before. They were not coming.

Things were going as badly for Fox as for Anderson. The seas were running so high that the sailors could not load provisions from the *Baltic* into small boats that would ferry them to Sumter. By noon, the *Pawnee* had captured a little schooner, which, Fox believed, could make a delivery run under cover of darkness. By 2 p.m. the *Pocahontas* had at last arrived and also a message that the *Powhatan* was not coming at all. Fox would have to make do without the *Powhatan's* guns and 300 fighting men and numerous assault boats. He could only hope that Anderson would somehow be able to hold out until nightfall.

That hope now appeared meager. The danger of fire spreading to the powder barrels in the casemate became so pressing that Anderson decided to throw all but five barrels into the harbor rather than risk an enormous explosion. Once more the exhausted soldiers rolled barrels by the score, this time to the open embrasures and into the sea. Yet once the barrels landed in the water, the waves kept them bunched dangerously against the base of the fort. Finally, a Confederate shell found them, touching off a loud explosion that did no damage except to fling an unmanned gun off its mounting inside the casemate. The men used sopping-wet blankets to shield what little powder remained from the sparks.

Nearly all the guns of Sumter were silent now, their crews barely able to breathe in the smoky air. Wrote Captain Doubleday, "The crashing of the shot, the bursting of the shells, the falling of walls, and the roar of the

Edmund Ruffin, the secessionist agitator who took part in the siege of Fort Sumter at the age of 67, sits for a victory photograph as a member of the Palmetto Guard—a South Carolina militia unit—six days after Sumter's surrender. A fervent rebel to the end, Ruffin committed suicide when the Confederacy fell.

flames, made a pandemonium of the fort." In the midst of all this, the thick mastlike flagstaff, already nicked several times during the bombardment, was hit once again and fell. Lieutenant Norman J. Hall raced out into the parade ground and recovered the flag, losing his eyebrows to the flames. He and Sergeant Peter Hart hastily improvised a flagpole, and then Captain Seymour led them in a dash to the parapet, where they affixed the staff to a gun carriage. The Stars and Stripes waved once more.

At last a breeze thinned the smoke, and Anderson ordered the men to increase their rate of fire. With the powder supply dwindling and no more cloth to make new cartridges, the workmen began sewing powder into socks donated by Anderson.

The Confederate gun crews, now sensing triumph at hand, redoubled their efforts, firing hot shot almost exclusively. Yet they admired the bravery of Anderson and his contingent, and when a shot came from Sumter after a prolonged silence, they sent up cheers and applause. Occasionally, the Confederates hurled epithets at the Yankee ships anchored out beyond the bar for failing to come to Sumter's aid.

When the flagpole on Sumter was knocked down, several Confederate officers concluded that the Sumter garrison was ready to capitulate. Beauregard ordered three aides to row out to Sumter and offer help in fighting the fire—his tactful way of telling Anderson it was high time to surrender. But someone else beat them there—with results that were nothing short of comic.

Former U.S. Senator Louis Wigfall, the Texan who had sent so much intelligence out of Washington, had arrived in Charleston and was serving on Morris Island as a volunteer assistant on Beauregard's staff. When Wigfall saw the Union flag topple, he decided that the fort had taken enough punishment. Moved by that sentiment and a chance for glory, he commandeered a small boat, drafted a South Carolina private and two slaves as oarsmen and started off for Fort Sumter holding a white handkerchief aloft tied to a sword.

It proved to be an exciting voyage. The little boat crossed the line of fire from Morris Island, passing just beneath the storm of Confederate shot and shell. It was almost hit by stray shots from guns on the other side of the harbor, where gun crews at and near Fort Moultrie could not see the boat. And it barely escaped errant shots from the smoke-blinded Federals on Sumter.

Incredibly, Wigfall reached Sumter without being detected by anyone in the garrison. He landed, strolled around to an open embrasure and showed his bearded face beside the mouth of the cannon—just as the gunners were preparing to touch off another round. Waving his handkerchief, Wigfall climbed in and politely asked to meet with Major Anderson.

While someone set off to fetch the major, Wigfall conversed with Lieutenant Davis. "Your flag is down," he stated, "you are on fire. Let us stop this firing." Wigfall offered Davis his white handkerchief. "Will you hoist this?"

Davis declined to do it himself but said that Wigfall could wave his handkerchief if he wished. He began waving it. Then a Federal soldier took his place and continued waving the handkerchief until a ball from Moultrie nearly hit him. By that time, Anderson had approached.

"I am Colonel Wigfall," the visitor announced. Then, having awarded himself a rank he did not hold, Wigfall opened wholly unauthorized negotiations: "Major Anderson, you have defended your flag nobly, sir. You have done all that is possible for men to do, and General Beauregard wishes to stop the fight. On what terms, Major Anderson, will you evacuate this fort?"

Anderson knew his answer. He was down to just four kegs of powder and three cartridges. Captain Fox's fleet showed no sign of attempting to come to his aid. The fire in the fort was still out of control, and his men were exhausted and hungry. He had done his duty and miraculously had not lost a single man. It was time to yield.

"I have already stated to General Beauregard the terms upon which I will evacuate this work," he said, referring to his last communication with Colonel Chesnut at 3 a.m.

The fiery trails of projectiles light up the night sky around Charleston as Fort Sumter, shrouded in smoke, duels Confederate gun batteries on the 12th of April, 1861.

the day before. "Instead of noon on the 15th, I will go now."

A little more talk settled the matter. Anderson's men could evacuate, saluting their flag and taking their side arms with them. Delighted with himself, Wigfall departed the island to report the surrender. At approximately 1:30 p.m., Anderson hauled down his flag and ran up a white cloth that somehow had escaped the attention of the cartridge seamsters.

All this byplay with flags was mystifying to Beauregard's three legitimate envoys, who were still en route from Moultrie to Sumter. They had started rowing when the fort's Union flag was shot down. They were halfway to Sumter when Seymour raised the Stars and Stripes over the parapet. Observing this, they turned back toward Moultrie, but then at 1:30 they saw the U.S. flag come down again and a white flag go up. Weary and confused, they pulled once more for Sumter and arrived shortly after Wigfall departed the scene.

The envoys—Captain Stephen D. Lee and aides William Porcher Miles and Roger Pryor—dutifully made their diplomatic offer to help Anderson.

Puzzled and annoyed by this second visitation, the major answered stiffly, "Present my compliments to General Beauregard, and say to him I thank him for his kindness, but need no assistance." Then he asked whether the envoys had come direct from Beauregard. Yes, they said. Anderson informed them that Colonel Wigfall had just been there "by authority of General Beauregard" and terms had been agreed upon.

The aides had no choice but to admit that Wigfall had no authority and had not even seen the general for two days. Indeed, they themselves were not authorized to give Anderson permission, as he now insisted, to fire a salute as he lowered his flag.

Anderson was enraged; having swallowed the indignity of surrender, he now gagged on the news that it did not count. "Very well, gentlemen," he said, "you can return to your batteries. There is a misunderstanding on my part, and I will at once run up my flag and open fire again."

Sensing that an opportunity was slipping away from them, the Confederates urged Anderson not to be hasty. They drew him aside to a casemate where they could speak privately and managed to persuade him to defer any action until they had explained the mix-up to Beauregard. At their request, the major wrote down the substance of his agreement with Wigfall.

Meanwhile, Beauregard, having seen the white flag go up, had dispatched a second set of aides with instructions to complete the surrender arrangements. These envoys arrived just as Lee's group was making ready to depart, and they offered essentially the same terms that Anderson had already accepted. And, at seven that evening, a settlement was reached that was as honorable as a surrender could be.

The Union garrison would evacuate the next day. The troops could fire a 100-gun salute to their tattered flag, and then they would be transported out to Fox's fleet for the trip home. Until then, the Federals would retain full possession of their fort—whatever was left of it. The Confederates had fired 3,341 projectiles during 33 hours of bombardment. All the barracks were in ruins. The main gate was gone. The outer walls had been pocked by hundreds of shells. Incredibly, only four men of the garrison had

been injured, each of them hit by flying bits of brick or mortar. The Confederates, too, had suffered only four men injured, all of them at Fort Moultrie.

That was all there was to it. "The men, released now from all responsibility, seemed to change in feeling," surgeon Crawford observed. "The enthusiasm that had so long inspired them seemed to have gone." There was nothing left for the troops to do but pack up their meager belongings and get ready to leave.

The Confederates rejoiced. The celebration started early in Charleston and the batteries all around the city. "A shout of triumph rent the air from the thousands of spectators on the islands and the mainland," wrote the 15-year-old Confederate Augustus Dickert. "Flags and handkerchiefs waved from the hands of excited throngs in the city. Soldiers mount the ramparts and shout in exultation, throwing their caps in the air." Beauregard sent a telegram to the Confederate government announcing the surrender, and copies were hurriedly broadcast through the Southern states. Cannon salutes were fired in the Confederate capital and 100 other Southern towns.

The Sumter garrison was ready to depart the next morning, April 14, 1861. Somehow the workmen had managed to sew together enough cartridge bags for the 100-gun salute. Major Anderson was seen in tears that morning, but he was grateful to his old friend Beauregard for allowing the salute. Grateful, too, no doubt, that the Confederate general had the consideration to refrain from setting foot on Sumter until after Anderson and his men were gone.

The salute began at about 2 o'clock that

afternoon. Thousands watched from boats in the harbor, among them Governor Pickens and Beauregard. Slowly the United States flag was lowered as the guns thundered on. Then Private Daniel Hough rammed another cartridge into his gun, apparently before sparks from the previous round were thoroughly swabbed out. A spark prematurely ignited the cartridge and the explosion tore Hough's right arm from his body. He died instantly.

The wind carried sizzling bits of cloth to the nearby stack of cartridge bags, and a second explosion mortally wounded another gunner and injured four others. Shocked by the double tragedy, Anderson cut short the salute at 50 guns.

Two hours later, with drummers beating time and musicians playing "Yankee Doodle," the men of Sumter marched out of the battered fort. Anderson tenderly carried the shot-torn flag, little suspecting that one day four years hence he would return as a general and once more raise that very flag over Fort Sumter.

The men of Sumter spent that night on board a steamer, the *Isabel*. Next morning the vessel ferried them out to Fox's U.S. fleet, and they were soon homeward bound aboard the *Baltic*. "Many an eye turned toward the disappearing fort," wrote surgeon Crawford, "and as it sunk at last upon the horizon the smoke-cloud still hung heavily over its parapet."

The guns had spoken. Like the sword that cut the Gordian knot, the Confederate cannon had sliced through the tangle of issues that reasonable men had failed to unsnarl for a half century and more. No longer would Northerners and Southerners have to grapple with the agonizing issues of slavery and states' rights, or with the rough-cut attempts to reconcile those issues. To the immense relief of many, the men of the North and the South were finally free to settle their complex differences in the simplest way— by force of arms.

"We are not enemies, but friends," Abraham Lincoln had told his countrymen, imploring them to listen to "the better angels of our nature" and remain friends. But those angels could no longer be of help, for now the Confederates and the Yankees were mortal enemies.

The Charleston Mercury Extra.

Saturday Evening, April 14, 1861.

THE BATTLE OF FORT SUMTER!

END OF THE FIGHT!

MAJOR ANDERSON SURRENDERS!

A special edition of the Charleston newspaper regales secessionists with stories of the surrender of Fort Sumter.

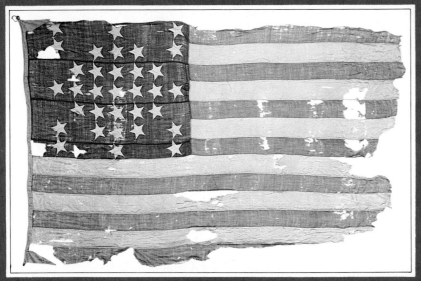

This United States flag flew over Fort Sumter
through most of General Beauregard's 33-hour
bombardment—until a Rebel shell shattered
its pole. Within 15 minutes, Federal troops had
raised the flag again by nailing it to a spar.
The nail holes appear along the left-hand margin.

Victorious Southerners stroll upon the esplanade fronting Fort Sumter in this composite photograph taken just after the Federal surrender. The walls of the f

A Change of Flags

ndreds of jubilant Southern patriots, ny of whom had paid as much as 50 cents ch for the pleasure, were watching from all boats in the waters off Fort Sumter as nion Major Robert Anderson struck his ttle-torn flag (*left*) and fired his cannon in emn salute. The withdrawal of the weary deral garrison went on at a funereal pace rough the early afternoon of Sunday, ril 14, 1861. Finally, after waiting chivously for two hours for the last of the nion soldiers to depart, a group of impor-t Southerners led by victorious General G.T. Beauregard put ashore at Sumter ittle after 4 p.m. and took possession the fort in the name of the Confederate ates of America.

The exterior of the fort was chipped and ted by Confederate cannon balls. But the mage to the façade was light compared th what the officers and politicians found en they entered the enclosed parade und through the sally port. Confederate

shells and shot, lobbed in by mortars and cannon firing at high angles, had exploded in the interior, setting fires in the officers' quarters and the enlisted men's barracks, strewing the parade ground with great jumbles of brick and masonry. The fires were still smoldering, and fire companies from Charleston would pump water into the ruins before the last embers died. Still, the wreckage inside Sumter looked much worse than it really was. Work parties began clearing away the rubble, and the fort would soon be ready to face far more ruinous bombardment by Federal warships.

For now, the Southerners were intent on enjoying their triumph. It had been an easy, almost painless victory, costing them only a few men slightly wounded, and when the Confederate flag and the palmetto-and-crescent flag of South Carolina were raised simultaneously above the fort, the celebrations that ensued were carefree and wild. Aboard all the sightseeing boats circling

Sumter, men and boys cheered, women wept, horns and whistles blew. The victory scene and the condition of the fort were recorded by photographers, who were kept busy by officials and soldiers demanding pictures of themselves for their memory books. Eager visitors poked about in the ruins looking for shell fragments to send as souvenirs to friends and relatives.

In Charleston, some three miles across the harbor, churches celebrated the victory with thanksgiving services. In St. Michael's Church, the Reverend J. H. Elliott recalled a Biblical battle in which the captains of Israel "fully achieved their object, and were now returned in safety to their tents without the loss of a single comrade." The pastor ended his sermon with expressions of gratitude for the Lord's mercy and bounty: "His Providence is fast uniting the whole South in a common brotherhood of sympathy and action, and our first essay in arms has been crowned with perfect success."

sides were pocked and cratered by more than 600 hits from Confederate gun batteries ringing the fort.

A cleanup crew gathers rubble at the damaged sally port inside Fort Sumter's main entrance. Behind the blackened brick wall at left are the burned-out officers' quart

Confederate dignitaries in top hats and frock coats inspect five columbiads mounted on the parade ground. These guns were under fire throughout the siege.

Jaunty Confederate militiamen strike poses beside the captured guns on the parade ground. In the background, at one of the corners of the fort, a stairway tower leads to the rampart.

From the barbette tier of Fort Sumter, Southern sightseers survey Charleston Harbor. The gun at lower left was bowled over by the recoil of the neighboring cannon, whose upended carriage lies at lower right.

Confederate soldiers man three guns on the parade ground as the Stars and Bars of the Confederacy (*above*) snaps in the breeze atop a derrick used to hoist guns to the fort's upper tier. The seven stars in the flag represented the Southern states that had seceded from the Union by the time Sumter fell.

ACKNOWLEDGMENTS

The editors thank the following individuals and institutions for their help in the preparation of the Civil War series:

Alabama: Birmingham—Birmingham Museum of Art. Mobile—Jay P. Altmayer; The First National Bank of Mobile; Caldwell Delaney, The Museum of the City of Mobile; R. Erwin Neville. Montgomery—Alabama Department of Archives and History; First White House of the Confederacy. Northport—Mrs. Ellis F. Cannon. Tuscaloosa—William Stanley Hoole Special Collections, University of Alabama Library; Jack Warner.

Arkansas: Jonesboro—Arkansas State University Museum. Little Rock—Robert Serio, The Old State House.

California: Los Angeles—Mamie Clayton, Western States Black Research Center. Redlands—Larry Burgess, Lincoln Shrine. San Marino—Carey Bliss, Alan Jetsie, Brita Mack, Harriet McLoone, Virginia Reuner, Huntington Library. Santa Barbara—Chris Brun, University of California, Special Collections.

Connecticut: Bridgeport—Bridgeport Public Library. Fairfield—Tom Lopiano Jr. Hartford—Connecticut State Library; Roberta Bradford, Stowe-Day Foundation; Edmund Sullivan, University of Hartford Dewitt Collection; Wadsworth Athenaeum; The Watkinson Library, Trinity College. Mystic—Mystic Seaport Museum. New Haven—Yale University Library. New London—U.S. Coast Guard Museum. New Milford—Norm Flayderman. Storrs—Mansfield Historical Society Museum. Wallingford—Wallingford Historical Society. Westport—William Gladstone, Ed Vebell.

Delaware: Wilmington—Delaware National Guard; Eleutherian Mills Historical Library; Historical Society of Delaware. Winterthur—Henry Francis du Pont Winterthur Library and Museum.

Florida: Bradenton—South Florida Museum. Ellenton—Judah P. Benjamin Confederate Memorial, Gamble Plantation State Historic Site. Fernandina Beach—Fort Clinch State Park. Fort George Island—Kingsley Plantation State Historic Site. Gulf Breeze—Gulf Islands National Seashore. Largo—Pinellis County Historical Museum-Heritage Park. Olustee—Olustee Battlefield State Historic Site. Pensacola—John C. Pace Library, University of West Florida; Pensacola Historical Museum; T. T. Wentworth Jr. Museum; West Florida Museum of History. St. Petersburg—Museum of Fine Arts; St. Petersburg Historical Museum. Tallahassee—Florida State Archives; Florida State Photo Archives; Florida State University Library; Museum of Florida History. Tampa—Hillsborough County Historical Commission Museum.

Georgia: Athens—Robert M. Willingham Jr., University of Georgia Libraries, Special Collections; Charles East, University of Georgia Press. Atlanta—Atlanta Historical Society; Tom Dickey; Beverly M. DuBose Jr.; William Erquitt; Georgia Department of Archives and History; The High Museum; Richard Kennedy; Richard Nee; Robert W. Woodruff Library, Special Collections, Emory University. Augusta—Augusta-Richmond County Museum. Columbus—Confederate Naval Museum. Crawfordsville—The Confederate Museum, Alexander H. Stephens Memorial. Fort Benning—Dick D. Grube, National Infantry Museum. Fort Oglethorpe—Chickamauga and Chattanooga National Military Park. Macon—Cannonball House. Marietta—Robert P. Coggins; Kennesaw Mountain National Battlefield Park. Richmond Hill—Fort McAllister. St. Simons Island—Museum of Coastal History. Savannah—Anthony R. Dees, Georgia Historical Society; United Daughters of the Confederacy Collection. Stone Mountain—Civil War Museum, Stone Mountain Park; Ralph Righton. Tybee Island—Fort

Pulaski. Villa Rica—Steve Mullinax. Washington—Washington-Wilkes Historical Museum.

Illinois: Cairo—Cairo Public Library. Chicago—Chicago Historical Society. Fort Sheridan—Nina Smith, Fort Sheridan Museum. Galena—Galena Historical Museum; Grant Home. Peoria—Peoria Historical Society, Bradley University Library. Rock Island—Dorrell E. Garrison, John M. Browning Memorial Museum. Springfield—Camp Lincoln; Rodger D. Bridges, James Hickey, Mariana James Munyer, Illinois State Historical Library, Old State Capitol. Wheaton—Du Page County Historical Museum.

Indiana: Bloomington — The Lilly Library, Indiana University. Fort Wayne — Mark E. Neely Jr., Louis A. Warren Lincoln Library and Museum. Indianapolis — The Children's Museum; Indiana Historical Society; Indiana State Library; Indiana War Memorials Commission. La Porte — La Porte County Historical Society. Notre Dame — The Snite Museum of Art, The University of Notre Dame; The University of Notre Dame Archives. Rensselaer — Jasper County Public Library. Vincennes — Jim Osborne.

Iowa: Des Moines—Iowa State Historical Society, Museum and Archives Division.

Kansas: Topeka—Kansas State Historical Society.

Kentucky: Frankfort—Linda Anderson, Kentucky Historical Society; Nicky Hughes, Kentucky Military History Museum. Lexington—Kent Masterson Brown; Hunt Morgan House; Frances Trivett, Waveland State Shrine. Louisville—The Filson Club; Frank Rankin. Perryville—Perryville Battlefield State Park. Radcliffe—Dr. Thomas Wheat. Richmond—Jane Hogg, Jonathan Truman Dorris Museum, Eastern Kentucky University.

Louisiana: Baton Rouge—H. Parrott Bacot, Anglo-American Art Museum, Louisiana State University; Beth Benton; Fred G. Benton Jr.; Dr. Edward Boagni; Shelby Gilley; M. Stone Miller, Main Library, Louisiana State University; Bill Moore; John E. Dutton, Rural Life Museum, Louisiana State University. Glenmora—Mrs. Francis Irvine. Mansfield—Greg Potts, Mansfield State Battle Park Museum. Natchitoches—Dr. John Price, Dr. Carol Wells, Louisiana Archives, Northwestern University. New Orleans—Barnard Eble, Pat Eymard, Confederate Memorial Hall; Charles Dufour; W. E. Groves; Patricia McWhorter, Kenneth T. Urquhart, The Historic New Orleans Collection; Mary B. Oalmann, Colonel Francis E. Thomas, Jackson Barracks; George E. Jordan; Vaughn Glasgow, Louisiana State Museum; Wilbur E. Meneray, Tulane University Library.

Maine: Augusta—Sylvia Sherman, Maine State Archives; Jane Radcliffe, Maine State Museum. Brunswick—The Hawthorne Longfellow Library; Elizabeth Copeland, Pejepscot Historical Society. Portland—Elizabeth Hamill, Maine Historical Society.

Maryland: Annapolis—Sigrid H. Trumpy, Alexandra H. Welsh, The Beverley R. Robinson Collection, The United States Naval Academy Museum; James W. Cheevers, The United States Naval Academy Museum. Baltimore—Donna Ellis, Paula Velthuys, Maryland Historical Society. Bethesda—Lucy Keister, National Library of Medicine. Boonsboro—Douglas Bast, Scoper House Museum. Clarysville—Clarysville Inn. Cumberland—Allegany Historical Society, Inc. Fort George G. Meade—David C. Cole, Fort Meade Museum. Hagerstown—Washington County Historical Museum. Sharpsburg—Antietam National Battlefield Center.

Massachusetts: Boston—Boston Public Library, Print Department and Rare Book Room; Commonwealth of Massachusetts, State Library; Francis A. Countway Library, Har-

vard Medical School; Craig W. C. Brown, First Corps Cadets Military Museum; Massachusetts State House; Cynthia English, Sally Pearce, Library of the Boston Athenaeum; Massachusetts Historical Society; Museum of Fine Art; Society for the Preservation of New England Antiquitie; James Stamatelos. Cambridge—Houghton Library, Harvard University; The Arthur and Elizabeth Schlesinger Library, Radcliffe College. Ipswich—Lewis Joslyn. Marblehead—Marblehead Historical Society. Newburyport—Historical Society of Old Newbury. Northampton—The Sophia Smith Collection, Smith College. Salem—Essex Institute; Peabody Museum. Springfield—Springfield Armory National Historic Site. Worcester—Higgins Armory; Worcester Art Museum; Worcester Historical Society.

Michigan: Ann Arbor—Mary Jo Pugh, Bentley Historical Library; John Dann, The William L. Clements Library, The University of Michigan. Detroit—Thomas Featherstone, Archives of Labor and Urban Affairs, Walter P. Reuther Library, Wayne State University; Alice Cook Dalligan, Burton Historical Collection, Detroit Public Library; Anita F. McCandless, Detroit Historical Museum; William P. Pheni Historic Fort Wayne. East Lansing—Frederick L. Honhart University Archives, Historical Collections, Michigan State University; William J. Prince. Kalamazoo—James Brady Jr., Paul DeHaan; Patricia Gordon Michael, Mary Lou Stewart, Kalamazoo Public Museum. Lansing—Ruby Rogers, Michigan Historical Museum, Michigan Department of State; John C. Curry State Archives, Michigan Department of State; Karl Rommel. Monroe—Matthew C. Switlik, Monroe County Historical Museum. Plymouth—Barbara Saunders, Plymouth Historical Museum.

Minnesota: St. Paul—Minnesota Historical Society.

Mississippi: Biloxi—Beauvoir. Clinton—Bill Wright, Jackson—Department of Archives and History; Patricia Cash Black, State Historical Museum. Natchez—The Historic Natchez Foundation; William Stewart. Vicksburg—Gordon A. Cotton, Old Courthouse Museum; Vicksburg National Military Park. Woodville—Rosemont Plantation.

Missouri: Blue Springs—Lone Jack Museum. Columbia—State of Missouri Historical Society; Western Manuscript Collection, University of Missouri. Independence—1859 Jail Museum; Jackson County Department of Parks and Recreation; Jackson County Historical Society Archives. Jefferson City—Missouri Department of Natural Resources; Missouri State Museum. Kearney—James Farm. Lexington—Battle of Lexington State Historic Site. Liberty—Clay County Department of Parks, Recreation and Historic Sites. St. Joseph—St. Joseph Museum. St. Louis—Missouri Historical Society.

New Hampshire: Concord—Mary Rose Boswell, New Hampshire Historical Society.

New Jersey: Camden—Margaret B. Weatherly, Camden County Historical Society. East Orange—Steven J. Selen friend. Merchantville—C. Paul Loane. Newark—Alan Frazer, The New Jersey Historical Society. Pittstown—John Kuhl. Ridgefield—Val J. Forgett. Trenton—Daniel P. George; Trenton Fire Department. Woodbury—Edith Hoelle, Gloucester County Historical Society.

New York: Albany—Gene Deaton, The Military Museum, State of New York Division of Military and Naval Affairs; Joseph Meany, Robert Mulligan, New York State Museum; Fishers—J. Sheldon Fisher, Valentown Museum. Hudson—American Museum of Firefighting; D.A.R. Museum. New York—The New-York Historical Society. Pattersonville—Montgomery County Historical Society. Peekskill—Memorial

Museum of the Field Library. Rochester—Janice Wass, Rochester Museum and Science Center. Troy—The Rensselaer County Historical Society. West Point—Marie Capps, U.S. Military Academy Library; Michael E. Moss, West Point Museum.

North Carolina: Carolina Beach—Chris Fonvielle, The Blockade Runners Museum. Durham—Robert Byrd, William Erwin, Ellen Gartell, Dr. Mattie Russell, William Perkins Library, Duke University. Kinston—Eugene Brown, Caswell-Neuse Historic Site. Kure Beach—Gehrig Spencer, Fort Fisher Historic Site. Raleigh—Dick Lankford, Division of Archives and Records; Keith Strawn, North Carolina Department of Cultural Resources. Southport—Colonel William G. Faulk, Ray Jackson, Fort Anderson Historic Site. Wilmington—Susan A. Krause, Bill Reaves, Janet Seapker, New Hanover County Museum.

Ohio: Cincinnati—Cincinnati Historical Society; First National Bank. Cleveland—Western Reserve Historical Society. Columbus—Ohio Historical Society. Coolville—Larry A. Strayer. Fremont—Rutherford B. Hayes Presidential Center. Hudson—Price Gibson; Thomas L. Vince, Hudson Library and Historical Society. Massillon—Margy Vogt, Massillon Museum. Mechanicsburg—Champaign County Historical Society. Sandusky—Follett House Museum. Sheffield Lake—William C. Stark, 103rd Ohio Volunteer Infantry Memorial Foundation. South Charleston—Jerry Rinker. Toledo—David Taylor.

Pennsylvania: Allentown—Lehigh County Historical Society. Carlisle—Randy Hackenburg, Dr. Richard Sommers, Michael S. Winey, Military History Institute. Enola—S. Craig Caba, Civil War Antiquities. Gettysburg—Gettysburg College; Gettysburg National Military Park. Gladwyne—Terry O'Leary. Harrisburg—Bruce Bazelon, William Penn Memorial Museum. Kittanning—Ronn Palm. Milford—Pike County Historical Society. North East—Irvin Rider. Philadelphia—Atwater Kent Museum; Free Library of Philadelphia; The Historical Society of Pennsylvania; Manuel Kean, Kean Archives; The Library Company of Philadelphia; Craig Nannos, First Regiment, Pennsylvania National Guard Armory and Museum; Philadelphia Maritime Museum; Russ A. Pritchard; The War Library and Museum of the Military Order of the Loyal Legion of the United States.

Rhode Island: Newport—Colonel James V. Coleman, Newport Artillery Company Armory. Providence—Richard B. Harrington, Anne S. K. Brown Military Collection; Jennifer B. Lee, John Hay Library, Brown University; Brigadier General John W. Kiely, Office of the Adjutant General; Providence Public Library; Joyce M. Botelho, Tom G. Brennan, The Rhode Island Historical Society Library and Museum.

South Carolina: Beaufort—June Berry, Beaufort Museum; Joel Martin. Charleston—Charleston Museum; Archives, The Citadel; Confederate Museum; Warren Ripley, *The Evening Post;* Martha Severns, Gibbes Art Gallery; Harlan Greene, South Carolina Historical Society; Julian V. Brandt III, Washington Light Infantry. Columbia—Fort Jackson Museum; Dr. Francis Lord; Laverne Watson, South Carolina Confederate Relic Room and Museum; Charles Gay, Alan Stokes, South Caroliniana Library, University of South Carolina; University of South Carolina McKissick Museums. Spartanburg—Robert M. Hicklin Jr. Sullivan's Island—David Ruth, Forts Moultrie and Sumter. Union—Dr. Lloyd Sutherland; Union County Museum.

Tennessee: Chattanooga—Chattanooga Museum of Regional History. Dover—Fort Donelson National Military Park. Franklin—Carter House. Greeneville—Andrew Johnson Historic Site. Harrogate—Edgar G. Archer, Abraham Lincoln Library and Museum, Lincoln Memorial University. Knoxville—Confederate Memorial Hall "Bleak House." Memphis—Eleanor McKay, Mississippi Valley Collection of Memphis State University; Jan Clement, Mud Island Mississippi River Museum; Pink Palace Museum; John L. Ryan. Murfreesboro—Stones River National Battlefield and Cemetery. Nashville—Belmont Mansion; Fisk University Library, Special Collections; Sarah and C. William Green-Devon Farm; Nashville Room, Public Library of Nashville and Davidson County; Tennessee Historical Society; Tennessee State Library and Archives; Tennessee State Museum. Sewanee—Jessie Ball duPont Library, The University of the South. Shiloh—Shiloh National Military Park and Cemetery. Smyrna—Sam Davis Home.

Texas: Austin—Eugene Barker Library, University of Texas; Confederate Museum; Texas State Archives. Mineral Wells—Mrs. Marjorie Cowan. San Antonio—William Green, Cecelia Steinfeldt, San Antonio Witte Museum.

Vermont: Bennington—Ruth Levin, Bennington Museum. Montpelier—Mary Pat Johnson, Vermont Historical Society; Philip Elwart, Vermont Museum.

Virginia: Alexandria—Wanda Dowell, Fort Ward Park; Boyhood Home of Robert E. Lee; Lee-Fendall House; Lloyd House, Alexandria Library. Arlington—Agnes Mullix, Arlington House, The Robert E. Lee Memorial. Fort Belvoir—

John M. Dervan, U.S. Army Engineer Museum. Fort Monroe—R. Cody Phillips, The Casemate Museum, Department of the Army. Fredericksburg—Robert Krick, Fredericksburg/Spotsylvania National Military Park. Harrisonburg—Scott Zeiss, Harrisonburg-Rockingham Society Museum. Lexington—Robert C. Peniston, Lee Chapel Museum, Washington and Lee University; Barbara Crawford, Stonewall Jackson House; Virginia Military Institute Library; June F. Cunningham, Virginia Military Institute Museum; Washington and Lee University Library. Manassas—James Burgess, Manassas National Battlefield Park. Marion—Marion-Smyth County Historical and Museum Society, Inc. New Market—James G. Geary, New Market Battlefield Park. Newport News—Lois Oglesby, Charlotte Valentine, The Mariners Museum; John V. Quarstein, The War Memorial Museum of Virginia. Petersburg—Christopher M. Calkins, Petersburg National Battlefield Park. Portsmouth—Alice C. Hanes, Portsmouth Naval Shipyard Museum. Quantico—Marine Corps Historical Center. Richmond—Dr. Edward Campbell Jr., Cathy Carlson, Museum of the Confederacy; Valentine Museum. Williamsburg—Margaret Cook, Earl Gregg Swem Library, The College of William and Mary.

Washington, D.C.: Oliver Jenson, Jerry L. Kearns, Bernard F. Riley, Library of Congress, Prints and Photographs Division; James H. Trimble, Audio-Visual Archives, Still Pictures Branch, National Archives and Record Service; National Portrait Gallery; Smithsonian Institution.

West Virginia: Weston—Jackson's Mill Museum.

Wisconsin: Appleton—William G. Phillip. Madison—Dr. Richard Zeitlin, G.A.R. Memorial Hall Museum; State Historical Society of Wisconsin. Menomonee Falls—Theodore S. Myers. Milwaukee—Howard Madaus, Milwaukee Public Museum; Gary S. Pagel.

Great Britain: Bath—Kay Bond, American Museum in Britain; James E. Ayres, C. A. Bell Knight, John Judkyn Memorial. Bury—Andrew Ashton, Bury Art Gallery. Kingston Upon Hull—Iain Rutherford, Wilberforce House. Liverpool—Janet Smith, Liverpool Record Office. London—Maureen Alexander-Sinclair, Anti-Slavery Society; Elizabeth Moore, *Illustrated London News;* Caird Library, Roger Quarm, National Maritime Museum.

The editors also thank the following individuals: Sacie H. Lambertson, Katie Hooper McGregor, Nancy C. Scott.

The index for this book was prepared by Nicholas J. Anthony.

PICTURE CREDITS

BIBLIOGRAPHY

Angle, Paul M., ed., Created Equal? The Complete Lincoln-Douglas Debates. University of Chicago Press, 1958.

Annals of the War. Philadelphia Weekly Times, 1879.

Bartlett, Irving H., Wendell Phillips: Brahmin Radical. Greenwood Press, 1973.

Basler, Roy P., ed.:
Abraham Lincoln: His Speeches and Writings. Gosset and Dunlap, 1946.*
The Collected Works of Abraham Lincoln. Rutgers University Press, 1955.

Bennett, Whitman, Whittier: Bard of Freedom. University of North Carolina Press, 1941.

Berger, Max, The British Traveller in America, 1836-1860. Columbia University Press, 1943.

Blassingame, John W., The Slave Community: Plantation Life in the Antebellum South. Oxford University Press, 1972.

Blue, Frederick J., The Free Soilers: Third Party Politics, 1848-1854. University of Illinois Press, 1973.

Boatner, Mark M., The Civil War Dictionary. David McKen Company, 1959.*

Bradford, Sarah H., Harriet: The Moses of Her People. Corinth Books, 1961.

Bragdon, Henry W., and Samuel P. McCutchen, History of a Free People. Macmillan, 1954.

Brewerton, J. Douglas, The War in Kansas: A Rough Trip to the Border. New York, 1856.

Buel, C. C., and Robert U. Johnson, eds., Battles and Leaders of the Civil War, Vols. 1-4. Castle Books, 1956 (reprint of 1888 edition).*

Burns, James MacGregor, The Vineyard of Liberty. Alfred A. Knopf, 1982.

Catton, Bruce, The Coming Fury (The Centennial History of the Civil War, Vol. 1). Pocket Books, 1963.*

Chadwick, John White, Theodore Parker: Preacher and Reformer. Scholarly Press, 1971.

Cole, Arthur C., The Irrepressible Conflict, 1850-1865 (A History of American Life, Vol. 7). Quadrangle Books, 1934.

Commager, Henry Steele, ed.:
Documents of American History. Appleton-Century-Crofts, 1958.
Illustrated History of the Civil War. Promontory Press, 1976.

Conrad, Earl, Harriet Tubman. Eriksson, 1970.

Cooper, William J., Jr., The South and the Politics of Slavery, 1828-1856. Louisiana State University Press, 1978.

Craven, Avery O., The Coming of the Civil War. University of Chicago Press, 1959.

Crawford, Samuel W., The Genesis of the Civil War: The Story of Fort Sumter, 1860-1861. Charles L. Webster and Company, 1887.

Cromwell, Otelia, Lucretia Mott. Russell and Russell Publishers, 1971.

Current, Richard N., John C. Calhoun. Washington Square Press, 1966.

Davis, William C.:
Breckinridge: Statesman, Soldier, Symbol. Louisiana State University Press, 1970.
The Deep Waters of the Proud. Doubleday and Company, 1982.
Shadows of the Storm (The Image of War: 1861-1865, Vol. 1). Doubleday and Company, 1981.

Dickert, D. Augustus, History of Kershaw's Brigade. Elbert H. Aull Company, 1899.

Donald, David:
Charles Sumner and the Civil War. Alfred A. Knopf, 1960.
Lincoln Reconsidered: Essays on the Civil War Era. Vintage Books, 1961.

Doubleday, Abner, Reminiscences of Forts Sumter and Moultrie in 1860-1861. Harper and Brothers Publishers, 1876.

Douglass, Frederick, My Bondage and My Freedom. Arno Press, 1968.

Duberman, Martin, ed., The Anti-Slavery Vanguard: New Essays on the Abolitionists. Princeton University Press, 1965.

Dumond, Dwight Lowell, Southern Editorials on Secession. Peter Smith, 1964.

Eaton, Clement:
A History of the Old South. Macmillan, 1975.
Jefferson Davis. The Free Press, 1977.

Edward, C., "Marats, Dantons and Robespierres," American History Illustrated, July 1977.

Elliot, Charles W., Winfield Scott: The Soldier and the Man. Macmillan, 1937.

Fehrenbacher, Don E.:
The Dred Scott Case. Oxford University Press, 1978.
Slavery, Law, and Politics: The Dred Scott Case in Historical Perspective. Oxford University Press, 1981.

Fite, Emerson D., The Presidential Campaign of 1860. New York, 1911.

Freeman, Douglas Southall, R. E. Lee: A Biography. Charles Scribner's Sons, 1934.

Gara, Larry, The Liberty Line: The Legend of the Underground Railroad. University of Kentucky Press, 1961.

Garrison, Wendell Phillips, and Francis Jackson Garrison, William Lloyd Garrison, 1805-1879, Vols. 1-4. Arno Press 1969.

Genovese, Eugene D., The Political Economy of Slavery: Studies in the Economy and Society of the Slave South. Random House, 1961.

Gilbert, Olive, Narrative of Sojourner Truth. Arno Press, 1968.

reene, Dana, ed., *Lucretia Mott: The Complete Speeches and Sermons*. E. Mellon, 1980.

underson, Robert Gray, *Old Gentlemen's Convention: The Washington Peace Conference of 1861*. University of Wisconsin Press, 1961.

Halsey, Ashley, *Who Fired the First Shot?* Hawthorne Books, 1963.

Hamilton, Holman, *Prologue to Conflict*. University of Kentucky Press, 1964.

Harrison, Lowell, *The Antislavery Movement in Kentucky*. University of Kentucky Press, 1979.

Heckmen, Richard Allen, *Lincoln vs. Douglas*. Public Affairs Press, 1967.

Heitman, Francis B., *Historical Register and Dictionary of the United States Army*. University of Illinois Press, 1965.

Helper, Hinton R., *The Impending Crisis of the South: How to Meet It*. Ed. by George M. Frederickson. Harvard University Press, 1968.

Henry, Robert Selph, *The Story of the Confederacy*. Peter Smith, 1970.

Holmes, Emma, *Diary of Miss Emma Holmes, 1861-1866*. Ed. by John F. Marszalek. Louisiana State University Press, 1979.

Holzman, Robert S., *Adapt or Perish: The Life of General Roger A. Pryor, C.S.A.* Archon Books, 1976.

Jenks, William (Williamson Jahnsenykes), *Memoir of the Northern Kingdom*. Boston, 1808.

Jenson, Merrill, *The New Nation*. Random House, 1965.

Johansen, Robert W., *Stephen A. Douglas*. Oxford University Press, 1973.

John Brown's Raid. National Park Service (Government Printing Office), 1973.

Jordan, Winthrop D., *White over Black: American Attitudes toward the Negro*. University of North Carolina Press, 1968.

Keller, Allan, *Thunder at Harper's Ferry*. Prentice-Hall, 1958.

Ketcham, Richard, ed., *The American Heritage Picture History of the Civil War*. American Heritage Publishing Company, 1960.

King, Alvy L., *Louis T. Wigfall, Southern Fire-Eater*. Louisiana State University Press, 1970.

Klein, Philip S., *President James Buchanan*. Pennsylvania State University Press, 1962.

Long, E. B. and Barbara, *The Civil War Day by Day: An Almanac, 1861-1865*. Doubleday and Company, 1971.

Lossing, Benson, *Pictorial History of the Civil War*. G. W. Childs, 1866.

Luthin, Reinhard H., *The First Lincoln Campaign*. Harvard University Press, 1944.

McCardell, John, *The Idea of a Southern Nation*. W. W. Norton & Company, 1979.

McPherson, James M., *Ordeal by Fire: The Civil War and Reconstruction*. Alfred A. Knopf, 1982.★

McReynolds, Edwin C., *Missouri*. University of Oklahoma Press, 1962.

Malin, James C., "John Brown and the Legend of Fifty-Six," American Philosophical Society, Vol. 17, 1942.

May, Samuel J., *Some Recollections of Our Anti-Slavery Conflict*. Arno Press, 1968.

Meier, Peg, ed., *Bring Warm Clothes: Letters and Photos from Minnesota's Past*. Minneapolis Tribune, 1981.

Mitchell, Betty L., *Edmund Ruffin*. University of Indiana Press, 1981.

Monaghan, Jay, *Civil War on the Western Border, 1854-1865*. Little, Brown and Company, 1955.

Moore, Frank, ed., *The Rebellion Record*, Vols. 1-12. G. P. Putnam, 1861-1868.

Moore, Glover, *The Missouri Controversy, 1819-1821*. University of Kentucky Press, 1966.

Neely, Mark E., Jr., *The Abraham Lincoln Encyclopedia*. McGraw-Hill, 1982.

Nevins, Allan:
The Emergence of Lincoln:
Vol. 1, *Douglas, Buchanan, and Party Chaos, 1857-1859*. Charles Scribner's Sons, 1950.★
Vol. 2, *Prologue to Civil War, 1859-1860*. Charles Scribner's Sons, 1950.★
Frémont: Pathmarker of the West. Frederick Ungar, 1961.
The Improvised War, 1861-1862 (The War for the Union, Vol. 1). Charles Scribner's Sons, 1959.
Ordeal of the Union:
Vol. 1, *Fruits of Manifest Destiny, 1847-1852*. Charles Scribner's Sons, 1947.★
Vol. 2, *A House Dividing, 1852-1857*. Charles Scribner's Sons, 1947.★

Nichols, Alice, *Bleeding Kansas*. Oxford University Press, 1954.

Nichols, Roy Franklin, *The Disruption of American Democracy*. The Free Press, 1967.★

Nicolay, John J., *Abraham Lincoln*. The Century Company, 1890.

Northup, Solomon, *Twelve Years a Slave*. Louisiana State University Press, 1968.

Oates, Stephen B.:
To Purge This Land with Blood: A Biography of John Brown. Harper Torchbooks, 1970.
With Malice toward None: The Life of Abraham Lincoln. Harper & Row, 1977.

Parrington, Vernon L., *The Romantic Revolution in America (Main Currents in American Thought*, Vol. 2). Harcourt, Brace, Jovanovich, 1955.

Pease, William H. and Jane H., eds., *The Anti-Slavery Argument*. Irvington, 1965.

Pfister, Harold Francis, *Facing the Light: Historic American Portrait Daguerreotypes*. Smithsonian Institution Press, 1978.

Phillips, Ulrich Bonnell, *American Negro Slavery*. Louisiana State University Press, 1969.

Population of the United States in 1860: The Eighth Census. Government Printing Office, 1864.

Potter, David M., *The Impending Crisis, 1848-1861*. Harper Torchbooks, 1976.★

Quarles, Benjamin:
Black Abolitionists. Oxford University Press, 1969.
Frederick Douglass. Associated Publishers, 1948.

Randall, J. G., *Lincoln the President: Springfield to Gettysburg*. Peter Smith, 1976.

Randall, J. G., and David Donald, *The Divided Union*. Little, Brown and Company, 1961.

Rawley, James A., *Race and Politics: "Bleeding Kansas" and the Coming of the Civil War*. Lippincott, 1969.

Roland, Charles P., *The Confederacy*. The University of Chicago Press, 1960.

Rudisill, Richard, *Mirror Image*. University of New Mexico Press, 1971.

Russell, William Howard, *My Diary: North and South*. Harper & Brothers, 1954.

Scarborough, William K., ed., *The Diary of Edmund Ruffin*. Louisiana State University Press, 1972.

Schaff, Morris, *The Spirit of Old West Point, 1858-1862*. Houghton, Mifflin and Company, 1907.

Sewell, Richard H., *Ballots for Freedom: Antislavery Politics in the United States, 1837-1860*. Oxford University Press, 1976.

Shaw, Albert, *Abraham Lincoln: His Path to the Presidency*. The Review of Reviews Corporation, 1929.

Sobieszek, Robert A., and Odette M. Appel, *The Spirit of Fact: The Daguerreotypes of Southworth and Hawes, 1843-1862*. David R. Godine, 1976.

Sorin, Gerald, *Abolitionism: A New Perspective*. Praeger Press, 1972.

Stampp, Kenneth M.:
And the War Came: The North and the Secession Crisis. Louisiana State University Press, 1980.★
The Peculiar Institution. Random House, 1956.★

Strode, Hudson, *Jefferson Davis, American Patriot*. Harcourt Brace, 1955.

Swanberg, W. A., *First Blood: The Story of Fort Sumter*. Charles Scribner's Sons, 1957.★

Swift, Lindsay, *William Lloyd Garrison*. G. W. Jacobs and Company, 1911.

Thomas, Benjamin P., *Abraham Lincoln*. Alfred A. Knopf, 1952.

Thomas, John L., ed., *Slavery Attacked: The Abolitionist Crusade*. Prentice-Hall, 1965.

Thomason, John W., Jr., *Jeb Stuart*. Charles Scribner's Sons, 1930.

Thompson, Robert M., and Richard Wainwright, eds., *Confidential Correspondence of Gustavus Vasa Fox*. DeVinne Press, 1918.

Thompson, William Y., *Robert Toombs of Georgia*. Louisiana State University Press, 1966.

United States Congress, *Congressional Globe*, 36th Congress, 1st Session, Vol. 1.

United States War Department, *The War of the Rebellion: A Compilation of the Official Records of the Union and Confederate Armies*. Government Printing Office, 1880.★

Villard, Oswald G., *John Brown, 1800-1859*. Doubleday, 1910.

Warner, Ezra J.:
Generals in Blue. Louisiana State University Press, 1964.
Generals in Gray. Louisiana State University Press, 1959.

Weiss, John, *Life and Correspondence of Theodore Parker*, Vols. 1 and 2. Arno Press, 1969.

Weitenkampf, Frank, *Political Caricature in the United States*. The New York Public Library, 1953.

Williams, Ben Ames, ed., *A Diary from Dixie*. Houghton Mifflin Company, 1949.

Williams, T. Harry:
P.G.T. Beauregard: Napoleon in Gray. Louisiana State University Press, 1955.
The Union Restored, 1861-1876 (The Life History of the United States, Vol. 6). Time-Life Books, 1980.
The Union Sundered, 1849-1865 (The Life History of the United States, Vol. 5). Time-Life Books, 1980.

Wilson, Forrest, *Crusader in Crinoline: The Life of Harriet Beecher Stowe*. Greenwood Press, 1972.

Wiltse, Charles M., *John C. Calhoun*, Vols. 1-3. Bobbs-Merrill Company, 1949.

Woodward, C. Vann, ed., *Mary Chesnut's Civil War*. Yale University Press, 1981.

Yearns, Wilfred Buck, *The Confederate Congress*. University of Georgia Press, 1960.

★ *Titles marked with an asterisk were especially helpful in the preparation of this volume.*

174